Author of Over 75 Books

PROMISES OF GOD'S GUIDANCE

God Show Me Your Ways, Teach Me Your
Paths, Guide Me In Your Truth and Teach Me

EDWARD D. ANDREWS

i

PROMISES OF GOD'S GUIDANCE

God Show Me Your Ways, Teach Me Your Paths, Guide Me In Your Truth and Teach Me

Edward D. Andrews

Christian Publishing House
Cambridge, Ohio

Christian Publishing House
Professional Christian Publishing of the Good News!

PROMISES OF GOD'S GUIDANCE: God Show Me Your Ways, Teach Me Your Paths, Guide Me In Your Truth and Teach Me by Edward D. Andrews

ISBN-13: 978-1-945757-87-7

ISBN-10: 1-945757-87-6

PROMISES OF GOD'S GUIDANCE

Edward D. Andrews

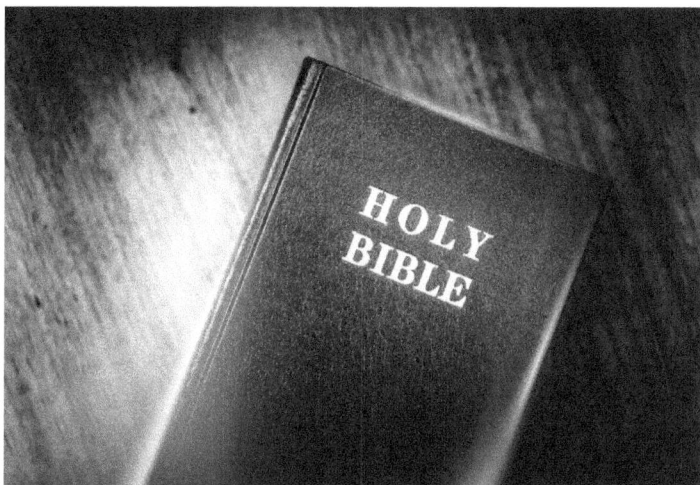

Table of Contents

PREFACE

Are we sure that we are truly walking in the truth? What kind of self-examination is fitting for servants of God? The Apostle Paul exhorted the Christians at Corinth to "Keep testing yourselves to see if you are in the faith. Keep examining yourselves!" (2 Cor. 13:5) Why should Paul's admonition to the Corinthians be of interest to us? We can do the same today. It will protect us from being uncertain as to whether we are walking in the truth. What standard do we have for testing whether we are in the faith, and why is that the perfect standard? If we are going to take a test to see whether we are truly in the faith, namely, truly walking with God, we must measure our conduct in light of the Word of God.

William Lange Craig wrote, "Remember that our faith is not based on emotions, but on the truth, and therefore you must hold on to it." What truth? Jesus said to the Father in prayer, "Sanctify them in **the truth**; your word is truth." (John 17:17) By identifying the Scriptures some of which actually say, "You are my disciples if ...," we can know if we are truly Christian. A test that can actually tell us whether we are walking in the truth should never be based on emotionalism, but rather on Scripture. Do our words, our thoughts, our actions, our mind, our heart attitude harmonize with the Scriptures? Within this publication, we will be able to let the Word of God prove who we really are. Let us follow the Apostle Paul's counsel, by testing ourselves to determine whether we are adhering to God's Word.

INTRODUCTION How to Recognize and Overcome Any Spiritual Weakness

2 Corinthians 13:5 Updated American Standard Version (UASV)

[5] Keep testing yourselves to see if you are in the faith. Keep examining yourselves! Or do you not realize this about yourselves, that Jesus Christ is in you, unless indeed you fail to meet the test?

When was the last time that we truly took a good look at ourselves? How did we feel about what we saw? When we ponder over our personality, what are we actually projecting to others? Most of us are very complex people when it comes to our thoughts, feelings, and beliefs so it might be difficult to lock down what kind of personality that we have. As a man, are we faithful like Abraham one moment and then blown back and forth like doubting Thomas the next? As a female, are we submissive like Sarah when we are in public and then like domineering Jezebel in private? As a Christian, are we devoted and energetic for the truth on Christian meeting days and then loving the world like Demas[1] the other days out of the week? As a Christian, have we entirely taken off the old person with its practices and clothed ourselves with the new person? – Colossians 3:9-10; Ephesians 4:20-24.

Some women are known to spend much time every morning, 'putting on their face,' as it is commonly expressed. So much so, it has been commonly joked about, and men know not to interfere until the project is over. However, truth be told, men are very much concerned with how they look when going out into public. Thus, all of us are conscious of whether our hair is out of place, if we have a pimple or a cold sore, or if there is something about us that is unkempt, ruffled, scruffy, or messy. We want to look our best. What we may have not considered is, our personality is always showing as well. The deeper question though is "are we putting on our personality to cover over before we go out in public while our real personality is on display in private?" Is what the public sees, who we really are? Does our real personality bring honor to God?

A man walking the roads of the countryside in a small European country comes to a fork in the road. He is uncertain as to which way he should go. Therefore, he asks several who are passing by for directions, but some told him to take the left fork, and others said to make the right. After

---

[1] A "fellow worker" with Paul at Rome (Col. 4:14; Philem. 24), who eventually, "in love with this present world," forsook the apostle and left for Thessalonica (2 Tim. 4:10). No other particulars are given concerning him. (ISBE, Volume 1, Page 918)

receiving contradictory information, he simply did not know what to do, how was he to go on, without knowing for certain which path led to the destination. He was unable to move on until he knew what the right path was. Having doubts about our faith, our walk with God, his Word can influence us similarly. It can actually cause severe emotional turmoil as we go about our Christian life.

There was a similar situation on the first-century Corinthian congregation. Some known as "super-apostles" were actually taking the apostle Paul to task, as to Paul's walk with God, saying, "His letters are weighty and strong, but his bodily presence is weak, and his speech of no account." (2 Cor. 10:7-12; 11:5-6) Certainly, we can see how a Christian in that congregation could wonder if they were truly walking with God when the apostle Paul himself was being called into question.

Paul founded the Corinthian congregation in about 50 C.E.[2] on his second missionary journey. "But when Silas and Timothy came down from Macedonia, Paul began devoting himself completely to the word, solemnly testifying to the Jews that Jesus was the Christ. And the Lord said to Paul in the night by a vision, 'Do not be afraid, but go on speaking and do not be silent; for I am with you, and no man will attack you in order to harm you, for I have many people in this city.' 11 And he stayed a year and six months, teaching the word of God among them." (Acts 18:5-11) The apostle Paul was deeply interested in the spiritual wellbeing of the brothers and sisters in Corinth. Moreover, the Corinthian Christians were interested in their spiritual welfare as well, so they wrote Paul for his counsel on certain matters. (1 Cor. 7:1-40) Therefore, Paul, under inspiration offered them inspired counsel in what would be his second letter to them.

"Keep testing yourselves to see if you are in the faith. Keep examining yourselves! Or do you not realize this about yourselves, that Jesus Christ is in you, unless indeed you fail to meet the test?" (2 Cor. 13:5) If these brothers in the days of having Paul found their congregation, who spent sixteen months under the guidance of the greatest, inspired Christian, needed to self-examine themselves, how much more should we need to do so, as we are 2,000-years removed? If these brothers followed this advice to examine themselves, it would have offered them direction on how to walk with God and let them know if they were on the right path.

Remember, Jesus warned, "Not everyone who says to me, 'Lord, Lord,' will enter the kingdom of heaven, but **the one who <u>does the will</u> of my Father** who is in heaven." (Matt 7:21) In other words, not every

---

[2] B.C.E. means "before the Common Era," which is more accurate than B.C. ("before Christ"). C.E. denotes "Common Era," often called A.D., for *anno Domini,* meaning "in the year of our Lord."

Christian was going to enter into the kingdom, even though they felt that they were walking with God. Jesus spoke of their mindset in the next verse, "On that day many will say to me, 'Lord, Lord, did we not prophesy in your name, and cast out demons in your name, and do many mighty works in your name?'" (Matt. 7:22) Yes, these ones, who felt that they were walking with God, on that day they were supposing that they were truly Christian, were in for a rude awakening. What is Jesus going to say to these ones, "And then I will declare to them, 'I never knew you; depart from me, you who practice lawlessness.'" (Matt. 7:23) What were and are these ones lacking?

Jesus said they were **not doing the will of the Father**, even though they believed they were. Notice that in 98 C.E., the apostle John, the last surviving apostle, in one of his letters offered that same warning too. He wrote, "The world is passing away, and its lusts; but the one who does the will of God remains forever." (1 John 2:17) Thus, we can see the wisdom of the apostle Paul's counsel to 'Keep testing ourselves to see if you are in the faith. Keep examining ourselves!' Thus, the next question is, what do we need to do to follow this advice? How does one test whether or not they are in the faith? In addition, what does it mean to 'keep examining ourselves after we have tested ourselves?

Keep Testing Yourselves

A **test** is a procedure intended to establish the quality, performance, or reliability of something or someone. In a **test**, there must be a standard by which something or someone is measured. For example, the "normal" human body temperature is 98.6°F (37°C). Therefore, if we were testing our temperature, it would be measured against the normal body temperature. Anything above or below that would be considered high or low. Another example is the normal resting heart rate for adults, which ranges from 60 to 100 beats a minute. However, our test in this publication is to see if we are truly Christian. However, what we are looking for when we 'test ourselves, to see if we are in the faith,' is **not** the faith, that is the basic Bible doctrines. In our test, we are the subject. What we are testing is, if we are truly walking with God. If we are to test our walk as a Christian, we need to have a perfect standard. Our perfect standard by which to measure ourselves is,

Psalm 19:7-8 Updated American Standard Version (UASV)

7 The law of Jehovah is perfect,
    restoring the soul;
the testimony of Jehovah is sure,
    making wise the simple.

[8] The precepts of Jehovah are right,
  rejoicing the heart;

Yes, the Word of God, the Bible is the standard by which we can measure our walk with God. On this, the author of Hebrews wrote, "For the word of God is living and active and sharper than any two-edged sword, and piercing as far as the division of soul and spirit, of both joints and marrow, and able to judge the thoughts and intentions of the heart." (Heb. 4:12) Thus, we must test our walk with God by examining our life course as outlined by Scripture, to find his favor, to be in an approved standing, to be declared righteous before him. Herein, each of the twenty chapters will have a text that they will be built around, a text that defines **what we should be** in the eyes of God. For example, several times Jesus says, 'if we are doing _____, we are truly his disciples.' Well, the objective would be to discover what all is involved in doing _____.

Keep Examining Yourselves

The phrase "keep *examining yourselves*" is self-explanatory, but it involves a self-examination. We may have been a Christian for a number of years, but how many times have we had a spiritual checkup. Every six months we are to go in for a dental cleaning and unless there is a problem, we should get a health screening once a year. The problem with our spirituality is it is far more susceptible to injury than we are physically. The author of Hebrews warns us, "We must **pay much closer attention** to what we have heard, lest we **drift away** from it." (2:1) One chapter later, we are told, "**Take care**, brothers, lest there be in any of you *an evil, unbelieving heart*, leading you to **fall away** from the living God. But exhort one another every day, as long as it is called "today," that none of you may be **hardened by the deceitfulness of sin**." (3:12-13) This same author warns us about falling away (6:6), becoming sluggish (6:12), and growing weary or fainthearted (12:25).

Why would this be the case? If we are saved, why is it necessary that we keep examining ourselves? Why would we still be susceptible to bad behaviors to the point of drifting away, to the point of having an unbelieving heart, falling away, becoming sluggish, growing weary or fainthearted?

There are four reasons. (1) First and foremost, we have inherited sin, which means that we are missing the mark of perfection. (2) In addition, our environment can condition us into the bad thinking and behavior. (3) We have our human weaknesses, which include inborn tendencies that we naturally lean toward evil, leading us into bad behaviors. (4) Moreover, there is the world of Satan and his demons that caters to these human weaknesses, which also leads us down the path of bad thinking and behaviors. After our self-examination, what is needed if we are to overcome any bad thinking or behaviors and how are we to avoid developing them in the future? We will offer more on this in each chapter as well as two appendices at the end, but we offer this for now. It is paramount that we fully understand what all is involved in our human imperfection and never believe that we are so strong spiritually that we would never fall away, slow down, or become sluggish in our walk with God.

Obviously, this should be of the greatest concern to each one of us. We may be a person of good character, and believe that in any situation, we will make the right decisions. However, the moment that **innocent appearing situation** arises, we are plagued with the inner desire toward wrong. We need to address more than what our friends, or our workmates or our spouse may see. We need to look into our inner self, in the hopes of determining, who we really are, and what do we need to do to have a good heart (i.e., inner person).

As we know, we could not function with half a heart. However, we can function, albeit dysfunctional, with a heart that is divided. Yes, we have things outside of us that can contribute to bad thinking, which id left unchecked will lead to bad behavior, but we also have some things within. The apostle Paul bewailed about himself, "For I do not do the good I want, but the evil I do not want is what I keep on doing. Now if I do what I do not want, it is no longer I who do it, but sin that dwells within me." (Rom. 7:19-20) This is because all of us are mentally bent toward the doing of wrong, instead of the doing of good. (Gen. 6:5; 8:21; Rom. 5:12; Eph. 4:20-24; Col. 3:5-11) Jeremiah the prophet informs us of the condition of our heart (our inner person), "The heart is deceitful above all things, and desperately sick; who can understand it?" These factors contribute to our being more vulnerable to the worldly desires and the weak human flesh than we may have thought. One needs to understand just how bad human imperfection is before they can fully implement the right **Christian Living Skills.**

Returning to the book of Hebrews, we are told, "solid food belongs to the mature, to those who through practice have their discernment trained to distinguish between good and evil." (5:14) We will have evidence that we are one of the mature ones by training ourselves to distinguish between good and evil. We likely believe that we are already spiritually mature, which may very well be the case. Nevertheless, we are told by Paul to carry out this self-examination and to keep on examining ourselves, to remain that way, and even to improve upon what we currently have by way of maturity. Just as a man or woman in a marathon must continually train their muscles to surpass others in the sport, our discernment (perception) needs to be trained through regularly and rightly applying the Word of God. Throughout this publication, we will apply the inspired words of James, Jesus' half-brother.

James 1:22-25 Updated American Standard Version (UASV)

[22] But be doers of the word, and not hearers only, deceiving yourselves. [23] For if anyone is a hearer of the word and not a doer, he is like a man who looks intently at his natural face[3] in a mirror.

[24] for he looks at himself and goes away, and immediately forgets what sort of man he was. [25] But he that looks into the perfect law, the law of liberty, and abides by it, being no hearer who forgets but a doer of a work, he will be blessed in his doing.

When we are inundated in the Word of God, it serves as the voice of God, telling us the way in which to walk.

Review Questions

(1) How can we test whether we are truly Christian?

(2) What warning did Jesus and the apostle John give to those who believed they were doing the right things?

(3) What is involved in examining what we ourselves are?

(4) Why must we keep testing ourselves?

(5) Why must we keep examining ourselves?

(6) Why do we need to understand just how bad human imperfection is before we can fully implement the right Christian Living Skills?

---

[3] Lit *the face of his birth*

CHAPTER 1 Putting the Father First in Our Life

Luke 14:33 Updated American Standard Version (UASV)

[33] "So therefore, any one of you who does not renounce all that he has cannot be my disciple."

Calculating the Cost

What did Jesus mean that we could not be his disciple if we do not renounce all that we have? Jesus had said just a few verses earlier, "For which one of you, when he wants to build a tower, does not first **sit down and calculate the cost** to see if he has enough to complete it?" (Lu 14:28) This section of Scripture is dealing with 'sitting down and counting the cost of what it means to be a disciple truly.' While this is not advocating that every Christian must reject all material things and live in isolation as early Christians thought, it is saying that if you are truly Christian, you must be prepared to give up all material things if that is what is called for in a particular situation. For example, suppose we had worked twenty years to build up a great Christian bakery and in the gay marriage climate of the recent United States Supreme Court, we were told by another court that we had to make a homosexual couple a wedding cake, which we had refused to do, or be arrested. What would we do? Would we risk our business that we sunk twenty years of our life into and share in the sins of others by making the cake? Our dedication that we made was to Christ Jesus not to material things. Thus, we must be prepared to 'renounce all that we have' if circumstances call for it or we are not Jesus' disciple.

Therefore, one who is truly Christian, i.e., truly a disciple of Christ, must have **calculated the cost** and have accepted that if there comes a time to **renounce all things,** God will not leave us in a lurch. While the salvation that Jesus offers all is freely given, there may come a time when being a disciple may cost us everything, including our lives, which God can replace, as in the case of Job. Again, leaving one's home, selling off all of one's belongings and giving it to some church, to live in some isolated commune, is not a qualification of being a disciple. However, we gave ourselves as slaves of Christ, meaning we have up our lives and all we own, and if, it comes to a circumstance where we must let our material possession go or be unfaithful, it means that we **renounce all that we have.** What we have is a loving relationship with the Father and the Son, salvation and hope of eternal life in the Kingdom of God.

Jesus gave his life on our behalf and for the Kingdom of God. When Jesus stood before Pilate, his life in the hand of this pagan, Roman Governor, he did not waver but stood there steadfast. (John 18:37) Even after being beaten to the point of death, hanging on the cross, he looked to the Kingdom of God, saying to one of the evildoers, "you will be with me in Paradise." – Luke 23:43.

Testify to the Truth

We need to ponder as to why Jesus focused so much attention and concern for the kingdom. Pilate said to Jesus, "So you are a king?" Jesus answered, "You say that I am a king. For this purpose, I was born and for this purpose, I have come into the world, **to testify to the truth**. Everyone who is of the truth hears my voice." (John 18:37) To what truth was Jesus testifying? He was testifying to the truth that the Kingdom of God would rule in righteousness and make it so that the will of the Father could be done on earth as it had been done in heaven. (Matt. 6:10) There is no greater joy than using one's life to help the Father in carrying out his will for humanity, bringing about pure worship earth wide.

The prophet Daniel foretold, "And **in the days of those kings** the God of heaven will set up a kingdom that shall never be destroyed, nor shall the kingdom be left to another people. It shall break in pieces all **these kingdoms** and bring them to an end, and it shall stand forever." (Dan. 2:44) The Father was to establish the Kingdom and the rule of Christ at Jesus second coming, and it would be **in the days of those kings**. What **kings** was Daniel referring to in his prophetic interpretation of King Nebuchadnezzar's dream? Some say Daniel was referring to rulers associated with the ancient Roman Empire, while others believe the kings are the four kingdoms pictured by the statue (i.e., the Babylonian, Persian, Grecian, and Roman empires), still others argue that the kings are from the Greek period, namely, the Seleucids and Ptolemies. Others would argue that Daniel is referring to the Maccabean period where the descents of Mattathias restored pure worship for a time in Israel.

Actually, all of these are wrong. Let us establish the points of the text.

- "In the days of those **kings**" refers to more than one king ruling as a world power because it is plural, i.e., more than one.

- "It shall break in pieces all these **kingdoms**" refers to more than one kingdom also holding sway in the world.

- "In the days of **those** kings," the demonstrative pronoun "those" refers to its immediate antecedent, namely, the kings within the statue.

Everyone agrees, "The God of heaven [the Father] will set up a kingdom [ruled by Christ at his second coming] that shall never be destroyed." How can this be, as the Babylonian, Persian, Grecian, and

Roman empires have passed away as world powers? Well, some might take the whole of that statue as the immediate antecedent of the demonstrative pronoun "those" but that is not necessary, nor could it be maintained or defended. Let us look at Daniel 2:32-33, which summarize the statue.

- **BABYLONIAN EMPIRE:** The head of this image was of fine gold,

- **MEDO-PERSIAN EMPIRE:** its chest and arms of silver,

- **GREECIAN EMPIRE:** its middle and thighs of bronze,

- **ROMAN EMPIRE:** its legs of iron,

- **CONTEMPORANEOUS EMPIRES:** its feet partly of iron and partly of clay

Old Testament Bible scholar, John F Walvoord writes, "The fourth kingdom in Nebuchadnezzar's dream represented by the legs and feet of the image is obviously the most important. Daniel gives more attention to this fourth kingdom than to the preceding kingdoms put together."[4] Can we see the mistake he is making? Daniel sections this statue not into four parts, but into five parts. First, let us say there are four chapters in the book of Daniel that have world powers moving through time, creating a timeline that walks us up to the Kingdom of God. These chapters intertwine and are in perfect harmony as to the world leaders on the stage.

CHAPTER 2 THE IMMENSE STATUE (Daniel 2:31-45): The head of gold is Babylonia. The chest and arms of silver is the Medo-and Persia. The middle and thighs of bronze is Greece. The legs of Iron represent Rome.

CHAPTER 7 THE FOUR BEATS (Daniel 7:3-8, 7, and 25): The first beat is Babylonia, the second beast is Medo-and Persia, the third beast is Greece, and the fourth beast is Rome.

CHAPTER 8 VISION OF A RAM, A GOAT AND LITTLE HORN (Daniel 8:1-25): Daniel himself tells us the interpretation, "As for the ram that you saw with the two horns, these are the kings of Media and Persia. And the goat is the king of Greece." (8:20-21) The controversy of this chapter is over the "little horn" that grew out one of the four horns mentioned in verse 8.

CHAPTER 11 KING OF THE NORTH AND KING OF THE SOUTH (Daniel 11:5-45): In Daniel chapter 11 we start with Daniel 11:2, which also begin with Persia and Greece. "And now I will show you the truth. Behold, three more kings shall arise in Persia [(1) Cyrus the Great, (2) Cambyses II,

---

[4] Walvoord, John F (2012-02-01). *Daniel (The John Walvoord Prophecy Commentaries)* (Kindle Locations 1460-1461). Moody Publishers. Kindle Edition.

and (3) Darius I], and a fourth [Xerxes I] shall be far richer than all of them. And when he has become strong through his riches, he shall stir up all against the kingdom of Greece." Then Daniel 11:3 reads, "Then a mighty king shall arise [Alexander the Great], who shall rule with great dominion and do as he wills." Daniel 11:4 reads, "And as soon as he has arisen, his kingdom shall be broken and divided toward the four winds of heaven [Alexander's four general split the territory[5] after Alexander died suddenly], but not to his posterity, nor according to the authority with which he ruled, for his kingdom shall be plucked up and go to **others besides these.**"

Now, Daniel 11:5-6 jump into a battle between the king of the south and the king of the north. Notice that Daniel had told us the four parts of Alexander's kingdom would **not be** a strong as his. That was true, as two of the four generals defeat the other two, leaving Ptolemy to the south and Seleucus to the north. The Ptolemaic and Seleucid dynasties were north and south of what? They were north and south of Israel. These two dynasties would go on for a time before being replaced by a new King of the north and king of the south. The king of the north and the king of the south run all the way down until the second coming of Christ, with one being the lead power for a time, followed by the other taking the power for a time. At his second coming, Jesus, the king of the Kingdom of God will crush whoever is the leading one at time, along with the contemporaneous empires (feet partly of iron and partly of clay). We return to Daniel 2:34, which read, "As you looked, a stone was cut out by no human hand, and it struck the image on its feet of iron and clay, and broke them in pieces." Notice that it was not the head of this statue, nor the chest and arms, or the middle and thighs, or the legs that were to be struck, but rather, it was feet partly of iron and partly of clay, i.e., contemporaneous empires and the king of the north and the south. The *feet partly of iron and partly of clay* is the immediate antecedent of the demonstrative pronoun "those," which refers to the contemporary empires or kingdoms that would rule in the last days, and would be destroyed by the Kingdom of God.

Yes, Daniel 2:45 would seem to shatter all of this because it reads "just as you saw that a stone [the Messianic Kingdom] was cut from a mountain by no human hand [but rather by divine power], and that it broke in pieces the iron, the bronze, the clay, the silver, and the gold. A great God has made known to the king what shall be after this. The dream is certain, and its interpretation sure." Even though the Babylonian (gold), Persian (silver), Grecian (bronze), and Roman empires (iron) had passed away as world powers, their remnants are still in existence today, and they make up

---

[5] Cassander ruled Macedonia and Greece. Lysimachus was over Asia Minor and Thrace. Seleucus I Nicator ruled Mesopotamia and Syria. In addition, Ptolemy Lagus ruled Egypt and Palestine.

contemporary empires, with the king of the north embarking on its final campaign "to destroy and devote many to destruction." – Daniel 11:44.

In the Gospel of Luke, an angel named Gabriel said to Mary, the mother of Jesus, "Do not be afraid, Mary, for you have found favor with God. And behold, you will conceive in your womb and bear a son, and you shall call his name Jesus. He will be great and will be called the Son of the Most High. And the Lord God will give to him the throne of his father David, and he will reign over the house of Jacob forever, and of his kingdom there will be no end." (Luke 1:30-33) This is very similar to the prophetic message from Daniel. The Father promised that Jesus would become the King of His Kingdom. During Jesus' life and ministry here on earth, he showed that he would be a kind, just, and perfect Ruler.

When Jesus ascended back to heaven, he was enthroned as King of God's Kingdom right away. However, he did not and has not for some 2,000 years broken into pieces all these kingdoms to an end and has not ended Satan's rule. The apostle Paul tells us, "But when Christ had offered for all time a single sacrifice for sins, he sat down at the right hand of God, **waiting from that time** until his enemies should be made a footstool for his feet." (Heb. 10:12-13)[6]

On these verses, Thomas D. Lea writes, "Two features showed the conclusive nature of Christ's sacrifice. First, Christ had offered only a single sacrifice, and this single offering did the job (v. 10). Second, Jesus' job as sacrificial lamb was finished. When Jesus exclaimed, "It is finished" (John 19:30), he really meant it. His enthronement at the right hand of God showed the completion of the task. His seat at God's right hand showed that God had exalted him to the position of highest glory. In Jesus, believers have access to unlimited grace and power. The present era is a waiting period as Christ anticipates a final victory over his enemies. We have been living in this era since the time of Jesus' exaltation to heaven. Christ has already won the victory, but we do not yet see the complete defeat of Christ's spiritual enemies. Rather than complaining about the delay, we should see this time as a day of grace to allow outsiders to experience God's mercy and forgiveness. We have no doubt or question about the ultimate outcome. Although this verse [10:12-13] does not directly quote Psalm 110:1 (see Heb. 1:13), that passage is clearly in view. Jesus is portrayed as our High Priest, assuming the kingship. As a king, Christ will enjoy full victory over his enemies. He will make a final display of triumph over evil at the end of history (see 1 Cor. 15:22–28)." (Lea 1999, p. 184)

---

[6] Who Authored the Book of Hebrews: A Defense for Pauline Authorship

https://christianpublishinghouse.co/2016/11/02/who-authored-the-book-of-hebrews-a-defense-for-pauline-authorship/

I would like to qualify Dr. Lea's last comment, which says, "He [Jesus] will make a final display of triumph over evil at the end of history." This does not mean the earth is being destroyed, just that the wicked are being destroyed and Satan and his demons will be abyssed for a thousand years. The original intention of the Father for the earth, righteousness will be realized and all of humanity, who will then be in perfection, will accept the sovereignty of God. Since 33 C.E., Jesus has ruled in heaven as the Father's appointed King. The Father and the Son have also selected some faithful men and women from the earth to go to heaven. They will rule with Jesus as kings, judges, and priests over humankind. Jesus said to his apostle, "You are those who have stayed with me in my trials, and I assign to you, as my Father assigned to me, a kingdom, that you may eat and drink at my table in my kingdom and sit on thrones judging ..." (Lu 22:28-30, ESV) On Jesus co-rulers, the apostle John wrote, "Worthy are you [Jesus] to take the scroll and to open its seals, for you were slain, and purchased for God with your blood men from every tribe and language and people and nation, and you have made them a kingdom and priests to our God, and they shall reign over the earth."[7] – Revelation 5:9-10.

One day soon Jesus will judge humanity, separating the like a shepherd separates sheep from goats. The sheep are those who are truly Christian. They have evidence that they have s genuine faith. They have been loyal subjects to the king and his kingdom. They will receive eternal life on earth, which will be ruled over by Jesus and his kingdom of co-rulers. The goats on the other hand will be those who have rejected Jesus Christ. (Matt. 25:31-34, 46) What are to happen to the goat like ones? Jesus and his co-rulers will destroy these ones. The apostle Paul answers,

2 Thessalonians 1:5-9 Updated American Standard Version (UASV)

[5] This is evidence of the righteous judgment of God, that you may be considered worthy of the kingdom of God, for which you are also suffering. [6] since indeed God considers it just to repay with affliction those who afflict you, [7] and to give relief to you who are afflicted along with us when the Lord Jesus will be revealed from heaven with His mighty angels in flaming fire, [8] in flaming fire, inflicting vengeance on **those who do not know** God and on **those who do not obey** the gospel of our Lord Jesus. [9] **These ones will pay the penalty of** eternal destruction, from before the Lord[8] and from the glory of his strength,

---

[7] **Resurrection Hope**

https://christianpublishinghouse.co/2016/10/15/the-hope-of-a-resurrection-where/

[8] Lit *from before the face of the Lord*

Do Not Be Anxious

Certainly, living in Satan's world that caters to the imperfect human flesh is no easy task. Jesus said, "I tell you, do not be anxious about your life." (Matt. 6:25, ESV) What should be our main focus? Jesus said, "Seek first the kingdom of God and his righteousness, and all these things will be added to you. Therefore, do not be anxious about tomorrow, for tomorrow will be anxious for itself. Sufficient for the day is its own trouble." (Matt. 6:33-34) Jesus set the example of putting the kingdom first in his life, and it was no easy task for him either. Those who are truly Christian will have to prioritize their life, knowing that each of us has different responsibilities, so not everyone can give as much of themselves to the kingdom as another. Therefore, we should not compare ourselves to anyone else. Jane might be a single mother with four children, while Lisa has a husband to help with only two children. John might be eighty-four years old, while Kenney is only twenty-three years old. Samantha and her husband might be living in poverty, while Denise and her husband are upper middle class.

Walking in the footsteps of Jesus means that we are willing to carry a cross and all that might be involved in being a disciple. If we are counting the cost of our service, this means that we are prepared to give up any material possessions for the kingdom. Lu 14:27-28, 33) No matter the events of our country, those who are truly Christian are obligated to share the good news with others, whenever the opportunity presents itself. The hope of attaining eternal life under the kingdom of Christ is what helps us to keep our focus, as we keep our eyes on the prize. – Matthew 13:44-46.

We must ask ourselves, 'do we allow secular activities to crowd out our service to God. Have we taken a job promotion that causes us to miss more of our Christian meetings? Do we skip our daily personal Bible study to do things with friends? Are we working voluntary overtime, which keeps us from the meetings? Are we considering a job that would mean we miss weekly meetings and our personal Bible study (e.g., truck driver)? We should do everything within our power to have a daily Bible study program, attend every meeting each week, to prepare for those meetings, to be able to participate, and to have some share in preaching the gospel to unbelievers. (Col. 3:23-24) Yes, if a family is in poverty, a father or mother needs to take whatever job can pull them out of poverty. Jesus does not expect us to leave our children in poverty because we are zealous for the kingdom. However, if we have to take a job that cuts into our worship, we should keep our eye out for another that will not cause us to set aside our worship. The congregation is strengthened by the presence of all of us.

Plan Ahead

Those who are truly Christian would do well to **live as though** Jesus second coming is tomorrow [maintain righteous standing], **plan as though** it is 50-years away [prepare life so one can evangelize to the extent possible]. What about our young ones though who are soon to be out of high school. They should be planning now, and parents need to prepare them if they are going to go onto higher education. We have already discussed in our previous book (*Let God Use You to Solve Your PROBLEMS*)[9] of the liberal progressive professors that are more evangelistic about atheism than most Christians are about the kingdom. Thus, studying some apologetic material prior to attending college is highly recommended. Whether our young ones are going to college or not, they still need to maintain the same level of worship.

Satan's world has a way of sucking the vitality out of us if we are willing to slave for it, as opposed to slaving for Christ. If our children are heading to college, they must consider the debt, which if much is accumulated, it will take many years to repay such. Do they really need to attend a big named university for the name alone? This may mean the difference between $15,000 a year, as opposed to $65,000 a year. Consider what that means after 4-6 years of college and university. In addition, consider eternal life. If we truly believe in eternal life, what difference does it make after we are millions of years into eternity, looking back on these few decades of imperfection?

Review Questions

- What does it mean that we cannot be a disciple of Jesus unless we renounce all that we have?
- Why did Jesus focused so much attention and concern for the kingdom?
- Explain the four chapters in the book of Daniel that have world powers moving through time.
- When did Jesus begin to rule and what are we awaiting?
- What did Jesus mean by our not needing to be anxious and why not?
- How do we evidence that the kingdom is first in our lives?
- Why is it important that we plan?

---

[9] ISBN-13: 978-1-945757-86-0

CHAPTER 2 We Must Love the Lord

1 Corinthians 16:22 Updated American Standard Version (UASV)

²² If anyone does not love the Lord, **he is to be accursed.**

Here the apostle Paul places a curse on anyone who does not love the Lord. Likewise, in Galatians 1:9, Paul wrote, "As we have said before, so now I say again: If anyone is preaching to you a gospel contrary to the one you received, **let him be accursed.**" While Paul clearly knew that most Christians accepted the gospel and loved Jesus Christ, he also knew that false teachers, deceptive men, and liars had slipped into the congregation as well. He had warned the Ephesian elders, "Take heed to yourselves and to all the flock, in which the Holy Spirit has made you overseers, to care for the church of God which he obtained with the blood of his own Son. I know that after my departure fierce wolves will come in among you, not sparing the flock; and from among your own selves will arise men speaking perverse things, to draw away the disciples after them." (Acts 20:28-30, RSV) Paul is telling us that the Lord even curses people in the Christian congregation if they do not love him. Notice the motive of some deceivers is **to draw away <u>the disciples</u>** [i.e., Jesus' disciples] after them. Paul even prayed that these deceptive ones who brought trouble would be punished.

Your Love Is Important

Matthew 22:34-40 Updated American Standard Version (UASV)

³⁴ But when the Pharisees heard that Jesus had silenced the Sadducees, they gathered themselves together. ³⁵ And one of them, versed in the Law,[10] tested him by asking, ³⁶ "Teacher, which is the great commandment in the Law?" ³⁷ And he said to him: "'You must love the Lord[11] your God with your whole heart and with your whole soul and with your whole mind.'[12] ³⁸ This is the greatest and first commandment. ³⁹ The second, like it, is this: 'You must love your neighbor as yourself.'[13] ⁴⁰ On these two commandments the whole Law hangs, and the Prophets."

If the Pharisees were surprised by Jesus answer, Scripture does not say. However, it would not be unexpected if they were because they knew Jesus was a carpenter's son and had not attended the rabbinic schools, nor had

---

[10] I.e. an expert in the Mosaic Law

[11] This is a reference to the Father, I.e., Jehovah of the Old Testament

[12] A quotation from Deut. 6:5

[13] A quotation from Lev. 19:18

he studied under anyone like Gamaliel.[14] Therefore, they likely thought Jesus being called a teacher by his disciples was not to be taken seriously and they could easily trip him up. Anyway, Jesus knew that the most important aspect of pure worship was/is the love of God, even though the Jewish religious leaders of his day failed to display it. In the synagogue, the Shema (Deut. 6:4-9), the Jewish statement of faith was often recited.

Deuteronomy 6:6-9 Updated American Standard Version (UASV)

⁴ "Hear, O Israel! Jehovah our God is one Jehovah! ⁵ You shall love Jehovah your God with all your heart and with all your soul and with all your might. ⁶ These words, which I am commanding you today, shall be on your heart. ⁷ You shall teach them diligently to your sons and shall talk of them when you sit in your house and when you walk by the way and when you lie down and when you rise up. ⁸ You shall bind them as a sign on your hand and they shall be as frontlets bands between your eyes.[15] ⁹ You shall write them on the doorposts of your house and on your gates.

While it is true that burnt offerings and animal sacrifices were a major part of the Mosaic Law, it was the love that the servant had for his Creator that mattered.

Micah 6:6-8 Updated American Standard Version (UASV)

⁶ "With what will I come before Jehovah,
  and bow myself before God on high?
Shall I come before him with burnt offerings,
  with year-old calves?
⁷ Will Jehovah take delight in thousands of rams,
  with ten thousands of rivers of oil?
Shall I give my firstborn son for my transgression,
  the fruit of my body for the sin of my soul?"

---

[14] Gamaliel was a "Jewish scholar. This man lived in the 1st century A.D. and died 18 years before the destruction of Jerusalem in A.D. 70 by Titus, the Roman general. Gamaliel is mentioned in Acts 22:3 as the rabbi with whom the apostle Paul studied as a youth in Jerusalem. Traditionally Gamaliel is considered to be the grandson of Hillel, and was thoroughly schooled in the philosophy and theology of his grandfather's teaching. Gamaliel was a member of the Sanhedrin, the high council of Jews in Jerusalem, and served as president of the Sanhedrin during the reigns of the Roman emperors Tiberius, Caligula, and Claudius. Unlike other Jewish teachers, he had no antipathy toward Greek learning. The learning of Gamaliel was so eminent and his influence so great that he is one of only seven Jewish scholars who have been honored by the title "Rabban." He was called the "Beauty of the Law." The Talmud even says that "since Rabban Gamaliel died, the glory of the Law has ceased." (Elwell, Baker Encyclopedia of the Bible 1988, P. 839)

[15] I.e. on your forehead

^{8} He has told you, O man, what is good;
   and what does Jehovah require of you
but to do justice, and to love kindness,
   and to walk humbly with your God?

As Micah shows, the cost of the sacrifice does not matter if it is presented in love and godly devotion. One could offer tens of thousands of the most costly animal sacrifices, but if it is not done in love, it is to no avail, i.e., worthless. Consider the account of a poor widow's offering at the temple, Jesus pointed out that with her two small coins, she put in more than all those who are contributing to the offering box. For they all contributed out of their abundance, but she out of her poverty has put in everything she had, all she had to live on." (Mark 12:41-44) Her contribution was given out of love and godly devotion. Think for a moment, what has the greatest value to God is something that we all can possess, regardless of our situation, our love for him.

The apostle Paul importance of love and the superior love to the Corinthians. He wrote, "If I speak in the tongues of men and of angels, but have not love, I am a noisy gong or a clanging cymbal. And if I have prophetic powers, and understand all mysteries and all knowledge, and if I have all faith, so as to remove mountains, but have not love, I am nothing. If I give away all I have, and if I deliver up my body to be burned, but have not love, I gain nothing." (1 Cor. 13:1-3) Plainly, love is vital if we are caring out pure worship and are truly Christian. Moreover, without love, it is impossible to please God. However, what are some different ways can we express our love for God?

Showing Your Love for God

While it is true that love is an emotion and it is spoken of as though we lacked control over it. For example, people have said, "you cannot help who you falling in love with." However, love is far more, which is regarded as an action in the Bible. The apostle Paul refers to love as "a still more excellent way" and as something we need to "pursue." (1 Cor. 12:31; 14:1, NASB) In fact, those, who are truly Christian, are encouraged to "let us not love with word or with tongue, but **in deed and truth.**" – 1 John 3:18, NASB.

We are not to love the world. The apostle John writes, "Do not love the world nor the things in the world. If anyone loves the world, the love of the Father is not in him. For all that is in the world, the lust of the flesh and the lust of the eyes and the boastful pride of life is not from the Father, but is from the world." (1 John 2:15-16, NASB) The psalmist tells us the same saying that we are love God but "hate evil." (Ps. 97:10) Love moves us to be obedient. John writes, "For this is the love of God that we keep his commandments, and his commandments are not burdensome." (1 John 5:3) Then, there is the love of neighbor. Yes, we show love for God by expressing our love for our neighbors as well. Jesus tells us that we are to 'love our neighbor as ourselves.' (Matt. 19:19) While caring for the sick, the needy, and the unfortunate is quite virtuous, helping them to find the path to eternal life is what God expected. – Matthew 24:14; 28:19-20; Acts 1:8.

Jesus voluntarily because of his love for the Father, love for humanity, and simply what is right, 'found himself in human form, humbling himself by becoming obedient to the point of death, even death on a cross.' (Phil. 2:8) This is evidence of one's love for the Father. Paul showed that it was by obedient love that we could have a righteous standing before God. Paul wrote, "As through the one man's [Adam's] disobedience the many were made sinners, even so through the obedience of the One [Jesus] the many will be made righteous." – Romans 5:19, NASB.

Therefore, we demonstrate our love for God by being obedient. "This is love that we walk according to His commandments. This is the commandment, just as you have heard from the beginning that you should walk in it." (2 John 1:6) Our love also means that we desire his guidance in our lives. Those who are truly Christian know that the way of man is not in himself, that it is not in man who walks to direct his steps." (Jer. 10:23) Therefore, we 'received the word with all eagerness, examining the Scriptures daily.' In other words, we work in behalf of our loving prayers with the Father, by looking to the Scriptures, to see more fully what his will and purposes are.

As Jesus said, we need to 'love the Lord our God with all our heart and with all our soul and with all our mind and with all our strength.' (Mark 12:30) Such love originates from our heart, comprising our feelings, desires, and our mindset, and we passionately desire to please the Father. Our love also originates in our thinking abilities as well, for our godly devotion is not motived by blind faith. We know who God is: his standards, qualities, will, and purpose. We know that he is really trustworthy and true. We know and understand why he has allowed this temporary pain, suffering, old age and death of humanity. We know Him!

Why Do You Love God?

"God is love" and we were 'made in the image of God. Therefore, we naturally love fellow humans and especially our Creator. Of course, inherited sin has hampered this natural love for God and neighbor (more on developing this love below), yet it remains within each one of us. The sovereignty of God, the right to rule or the righteousness of God's rule is found in God's desire for us to serve him out of love not dreadful fear. In other words, we appreciate the life we have now and the life that is to come, and we love the righteousness of his rule.

If we are to love God to the extent that Scriptures show, he cannot just be some distant being outside of the created universe. He is a person, who is spirit (i.e., invisible), but a real person, who spent 1600 years, sixty-six book and forty human authors revealing his love for us. He brought Noah through the flood. He brought Abraham into the land that his descendants would own. He brought Moses and millions out of slavery in Egypt. He rescued his people from one threat after another, even though they were the most unruly child for more than a millennium. He even disciplined them in love. He sheltered, sustained, and cherished the Israelites. He even gave the only begotten Son as a ransom, so that some might be saved, so our faith and hope might be in Him. Thus, we love our Father and neighbor, because he first loved us. – 1 John 4:19.

Developing Your Love for God

The apostle John tells us "no one has seen God at any time." (John 1:18) This is because "**God is spirit.**" (John 4:24) Nevertheless, we are invited by James to 'draw near God.' (Jam 4:8) How is it even possible to draw near to an invisible spirit person? If we walk into a mall, there are hundreds of people walking around. Just because we can see all of those people, does that mean we love them? No. What is it that makes us love another person? It is by our getting to know him, right? As we get to know a new person, we draw close to them in friendship. Was not Abraham called God's friend? (James 2:21-23) The apostle John wrote, "This is eternal life: that they may **know** you, the only true God, and the One you have sent, Jesus Christ." The Greek (*ginosko*) behind our English "they may know," is referring not to head knowledge but rather indicates a relationship. Therefore, the more we know about the Father, and the Son and our love for them will develop over time.

When we watch a movie, we get emotionally involved with characters that we do not even know. However, as an avid book reader will tell you, a great novel will draw us into the lives of the characters and the plot even more than a movie. In a book, we see these characters through our heart, to the point that we will get angry or cry when a beloved character loses their life or is even spoken of in a disparaging way. We also find joy when our main character succeeds. We literally have four novels of the life and ministry of Jesus Christ.

Jesus tells us, "Whoever has seen me has seen the Father." (John 14:9) We could read the gospels through, where we would find the compassion that Jesus showed to a widow when he resurrected her only son. (Lu 7:11-15) As we work through the gospels, see the power, the strength, and wisdom of this one man, to find him washing the feet of his disciples. (John 13:3-5) Could we not draw close to such a great man, who also took out time to be with the children? (Mark 10:13-14) If we read the four gospels, we too can feel like those that Peter wrote to in his first letter. "Though you have not seen him, you love him. Though you do not now see him, you believe in him and rejoice with joy that is inexpressible and filled with glory." (1 Pet. 1:8) As our love for Jesus grows, so will our love for the Father. As we read the Old Testament, we will be emotionally moved as we draw closer to the Father, which means drawing close to the Son as well.

Paul tells us; God "did not leave himself without witness, for he did good by giving you rains from heaven and fruitful seasons, satisfying your hearts with food and gladness." (Acts 14:17, ESV) In a letter to the Christians in Rome, Paul writes, God's "invisible attributes, namely, his eternal power and divine nature, have been clearly perceived, ever since the creation of the world, in the things that have been made." Therefore, we have yet another way that we can develop our love for God. We can appreciate all that he has provided us, as well as the beauty of his creation, and how wonderfully we were made. Yes, we were designed to enjoy living in our earthly home but we also enjoy the beauty of it. For example, pondering the human eye alone can help draw closer to God.

Taylor Richardson writes, "For many years, scientists have compared the eye to the modern manmade camera (see Miller, 1960, p. 315; Nourse, 1964, p. 154; Gardener, 1994, p. 105). True, the eye and camera do have many things in common, if the function of the camera demands that it was "made," does it not stand to reason that the **more complex** human camera, the eye, also must have had a Maker? Alan Gillen explained it best when he wrote: 'No human camera, artificial device, nor computer-enhanced light-sensitive device can match the contrivance of the human eye. **Only a master engineer with superior intelligence could manufacture a series of interdependent light-sensitive parts and reactions**' (p. 99, emp. added). That master engineer was God. The writer of Proverbs knew this when he wrote, 'The hearing ear and the seeing eye, the Lord has made them both' (20:12)."[16]

The more we take in from his Word the Bible as well as the physical universe, the more we learn of God's endless goodness and generosity.

---

[16] Apologetics Press - Seeing is Believing: The Design of the Human Eye (accessed October 12, 2015).

http://www.apologeticspress.org/APContent.aspx?category=9&article=1412

Another gift that he has given humans is prayer. He could have just created humans, a far inferior creature than even his angelic creations, and he could have just left us to enjoy his creation. Nevertheless, he gave us a way to communicate with him, namely, prayer. He even went a step further and made prayer a part of our worship. God expects us in our private prayers to speak about whatever lies on our hearts, anything that affects our relationship with him. We can literally talk to God whenever our heart motivates us to do so. The only condition of being heard, we must be making some effort to carry out his will and purposes. The Father listens to every prayer and he knows each of us personally and intimately. King David said, "O you who hear prayer, to you shall all flesh come." – Psalm 65:2.

Once we fully accept the existence of God and the truthfulness of his Word, we can also draw close to him by considering what he has in store for humankind and our planet earth.[17] What can we learn from Scripture? God created the earth to be inhabited, to be filled with perfect humans, who are over the animals, and under the sovereignty of God. (Gen 1:28; 2:8, 15; Ps 104:5; 115:16; Eccl 1:4) Sin did not dissuade God from his plans (Isa. 45:18); hence, he has saved redeemable humankind by Jesus ransom sacrifice. It seems that the Bible offers two hopes to redeemed humans, (1) a heavenly hope, or (2) an earthly hope. It also seems that those with the heavenly hope are limited in number, and are going to heaven to rule with Christ as kings, priests, and judges either on the earth or over the earth from heaven. It seems that those with the earthly hope are going to receive everlasting life here on a paradise earth as originally intended. Ponder the words of Walter A. Elwell,

> In the O[ld] T[estament] the kingdom of God is usually described in terms of a redeemed earth; this is especially clear in the book of Isaiah, where the final state of the universe is already called new heavens and a new earth (65:17; 66:22) The nature of this renewal was perceived only very dimly by OT authors, but they did express the belief that a humans ultimate destiny is an earthly one.[15] This vision is clarified in the N[ew] T[estament]. Jesus speaks of the "renewal" of the world (Matt 19:28), Peter of the restoration of all things (Acts 3:21). Paul writes that the universe will be redeemed by God from its current state of bondage (Rom. 8:18-21). This is confirmed by Peter, who describes the new heavens and the new earth as the Christian's hope (2 Pet. 3:13). Finally, the book of Revelation includes a glorious vision of the end of the present universe and the creation of a new universe, full of righteousness and the presence of God.

---

[17] http://www.christianpublishers.org/resurrection-hope-where

The vision is confirmed by God in the awesome declaration: "I am making everything new!" (Rev. 21:1-8).

The new heavens and the new earth will be the renewed creation that will fulfill the purpose for which God created the universe. It will be characterized by the complete rule of God and by the full realization of the final goal of redemption: "Now the dwelling of God is with men" (Rev. 21:3).

The fact that the universe will be created anew[16] shows that God's goals for humans is not an ethereal and disembodied existence, but a bodily existence on a perfected earth. The scene of the beatific vision is the new earth. The spiritual does not exclude the created order and will be fully realized only within a perfected creation. (Elwell, Evangelical Dictionary of Theology (Second Edition) 2001, pp. 828-29)

Therefore, once we get to know God fully through his Word and his Creation, our love for him will grow to the point that we like Jesus, would lay this life down for him, knowing that we have a resurrection hope awaiting us. As we continue to grow in this life-saving knowledge, our love for God will only continue to be strengthened, especially as he directs and guides us through the landmines of Satan's world. If our love is to grow, it must be cultivated and maintained through prayer, personal Bible study, family study, preparing for our Christian meetings, telling others what we have learned, and enjoying the life that God gave us. Moses said some 3.500 years ago, "I call heaven and earth to witness against you today, that I have set before you life and death, blessing and curse. Therefore choose life, that you and your offspring may live, loving the Lord your God, obeying his voice and holding fast to him, for he is your life and length of days, that you may dwell in the land that the Lord swore to your fathers, to Abraham, to Isaac, and to Jacob, to give them." – Deuteronomy 30:19-20, ESV.

Review Questions

- Why is your love for God so important?
- How can you show love for God?
- Why do You Love God?
- How might you develop your love of God?

CHAPTER 3 Our Greatest Need Is Love

Mark 12:31 Updated American Standard Version (UASV)

[31] The second is this: 'You shall love your neighbor as yourself.' There is no other commandment greater than these."

The twenty-first century has become the "Self-First" generation. Nick Gillespie writes, "Seventy-one percent of American adults think of 18-to-29-year-olds – millennials, basically – as "selfish," and 65% of us think of them as "entitled." That's according to the latest Reason-Rupe Poll, a quarterly survey of 1,000 representative adult Americans. If millennials are self-absorbed little monsters who expect the world to come to them and for their parents to clean up their rooms well into their 20s, we've got no one to blame but ourselves — especially the moms and dads among us."[18]

The apostle Paul told the Ephesian elders, "In all things I have shown you that by working hard in this way we must help the weak and remember the words of the Lord Jesus, how he himself said, 'It is more blessed to give than to receive.'" (Acts 20:35, ESV) Kenneth O. Gangel writes about this verse, "Like Paul, the Ephesian elders should not covet material things nor expect such from the congregation. One can only assume that these were hardly full-time vocational pastors but lay leaders who served others through hard work. Paul's concern for the weak and the needy is well documented in his epistles (Rom. 15:1; 1 Thess. 5:14; Eph. 4:28; Gal. 6:2). He particularly turns to this theme in dealing with the elders (1 Tim. 3:3, 8; Titus 1:7, 11), perhaps because false teachers in Asia so frequently acted in greed and love of material things. Would God that modern church leaders, many of whom live in opulence far exceeding that of their parishioners and constituents, would pay heed to this simple teaching from Miletus. The greed against which Paul warned the Ephesian elders seems to be an assumed trait of many popular figures in the modern church." (K. O. Gangel 1998, p. 345)

The trend is toward selfishness today. Some young parents today will put drugs before their children. This author is aware of a young woman who did several thousands of dollars of heroin throughout her entire pregnancy. Her father pled with her about the dangers to the baby, and her response was frightening to say the least. This young woman's argument that the baby would be fine was that her young brother was healthy, as her mother had done crack throughout her entire pregnancy, and her brother

---

[18] Millennials Are Selfish and Entitled, and Helicopter Parents .., http://time.com/3154186/millennials-selfish-entitled-helicopter-parenting/ (accessed October 12, 2015).

came out fine. Well, the young woman lost her child to social services and had yet to get treatment for her addiction. In fact, she is pregnant again and still doing heroin. Sadly, this type of behavior by our young people is more prevalent than one might think.

However, there are some young people, who are exemplary in unselfishness. There are some young parents who are so devoted to their families that they sacrifice everything for their children. In fact, they have family and friends that urge them to get things for themselves or to have a date night, for they feel like their children must always come first. There are young women who have been left with several young children because the father died in a war, and they managed the households, worked more than one job, never getting anything for themselves, like new clothes, recreation, or going out on a date. These women were consumed with the need to provide their children a future. At the end of the day, lying in their beds exhausted, what reward did they have? They could feel the love and gratitude of their children, knowing that they had a future because of their mother. These parents saw the results when the report cards came home, or the children won some sports championship, or they received a scholarship to a good university. The mothers had the joy of giving rather than receiving.

We feel far more joy when we watch a loved one open our present, seeing the smile and joy on their face; than we do in receiving a present ourselves. Why? This is because our Creator made us in his image and likeness, and there is no one more selfless than he is. Our heavenly Father gave us an inner moral code, which enables us to determine what is right and what is wrong. However, he went a step further by also endowing us with the ability to feel good about justice. We feel happy, content when we do what is right, and it works out for the better in one's life.

Hence, the famed English jurist Blackstone stated that God has "so intimately connected, so inseparably interwoven the laws of eternal justice with the happiness of each individual, that the latter [happiness] cannot be attained but by observing the former [justice]; and, if the former be punctually obeyed, it cannot but induce the latter."[19] This is certainly true that we cannot have happiness without first having justice. Moreover, the same is true of selflessness. We cannot have true and pure joy and happiness without first living an unselfish life.

---

[19] The Pursuit of - Not the Right to - Happiness -- KEVIN CRAIG .., http://kevincraig.us/pursuit.htm (accessed October 15, 2015).

Godly Qualities versus Inherited Sin

It should be noted that the godly qualities that we have been by our Creator are in every one of us, even in our imperfection. However, we do have another inner desire that wars against our desires to follow the qualities that God has instilled in us. Because of our imperfection, we are mentally bent toward evil. (Gen. 6:5; 8:21; Ps. 51:5, AT) Moreover, our heart (inner person, the seat of motivation) 'is deceitful above all things, and desperately sick; which we cannot understand.' (Jer. 17:9) Therefore, if we are going to maintain and develop the quality of putting other people's needs, interests, or wishes before our own, we must cultivate our selfless side. This is especially true within the family because if one person is a selfish person, it will be a life of pain and suffering for everyone else. The reality is, it was the selfishness of Satan, Adam and Eve that has humankind living in imperfection, pain, suffering, old age and death. Sadly, every argument between family and friends, every conflict between leaders, every war between nations, every dispute between employer and employee, and every crime is the result of selfishness. Our concern with our own interests, needs, and wishes while ignoring those of others will ruin our life and any relationship we might ever hope to have.

What motivates us to be selfless? It is another human quality, empathy, the ability to identify with and understand somebody else's feelings or difficulties. When we do something for another, like pay for a military person's meal at a restaurant, we are empathizing with what he gave up, so we have the freedom we have. This brings us to another quality, gratitude, i.e., being thankful for what others have done. Imagine, the traffic is moving slowly, and we are laying on our horn because we are in a hurry. Soon, we see several ambulances ahead. As we drive by a car wreck, we see a teenage girl being zipped up in a black body bag. Suddenly, our heart is beating heavily; we feel the pain of that child, the pain of the mother, and our being late for a meeting is the furthest thing from our mind. If we have never pondered whether we carry out selfless acts, we might start with something small. We might focus on getting the door for people, offering better tips for service, helping someone in a small way, considering how others might feel, and seeing how we react to inconveniences. When we see how others react to our small acts of kindness, will help us to develop our selfless side further.

The apostle Paul wrote, "Let no one seek his own good, but the good of his neighbor." (1 Cor. 10:24, ESV) On this verse, Bible scholar David E. Garland writes, "Paul's command that one "not seek that which is one's own" leaves indefinite what they are not to seek.[3] We can fill in the blank with words such as "advantage," "interest," "good," "ends," "enjoyment," "needs." Instead of selfish things, they are to seek the interests of the other … This "other" is not restricted to the fellow believer who might have a weak conscience, as in 8:11, but also includes the unbeliever who might offer an invitation to dinner (10:27). His concern in this section is not the effect of their behavior on other believers but its effect on nonbelievers. The overarching hermeneutical principles that govern his practical advice are these: What course of action will bring glory to God, and what course of action will be "the most effective witness to Christ?" (Ruef 1977: 103). Paul expects the Corinthians to do all things to bring glory to God (10:31) and to seek the best interests of others so that they might be saved (10:33)." (Garland 2003, p. 489)

Jesus' half-brother James wrote, "Religion that is pure and undefiled before God, the Father, is this: to visit orphans and widows in their affliction, and to keep oneself unstained from the world." (Jam. 1:27, ESV) On this, the *CPH New Testament Commentary* says, "James specifically mentions that these people were to be visited in their times of distress. The word in Greek used here for distress is *thlipsis,* and it means 'pressure or a pressing together.' (Vine, 1996, pg. 17) James is not saying they were to be helped when they had no more troubles, but rather it was *in the midst of* their troubles. They were to be helped as they were going through the pressures of life that were coming against them. This could include clothing, feeding, and giving them shelter, and show the love of Christ to them. James echoes what John wrote in I John 3:16-18, 'We know love by this, that He laid down His life for us; and we ought to lay down our lives for the brethren. But whoever has the world's goods, and sees his brother in need and closes his heart against him, how does the love of God abide in him? Little children, let us not love with word or with tongue, but in deed and truth.' Several Scriptures point to the fact that God has a great concern for the orphans and widows.[20]" (Calloway 2015, p. 44)

There is little doubt that world of humankind alienated from God has entered its most selfish era in its history. While every human would say they want joy and happiness in their life, yet most are seeking to receive as opposed to giving. The reality is that we can never have true happiness and joy without developing the mentality of being selfless from the heart. This means that we are selfless; we do good to others naturally, as each and every opportunity presents itself. We do these things to family, friends, coworkers, neighbors, strangers, and even our enemies. Our greatest joy comes from sharing the good news with others, helping someone to cross over from death to life. Jesus said, "Truly, truly, I say to you, whoever hears my word and believes him who sent me has eternal life. He does not come into judgment, but has passed from death to life." (John 5:24, ESV; See 1

---

[20] See Deuteronomy 10:18; 14:28–29; 16:11; 24:17; 26:12; Jeremiah 22:3; Zechariah 7:8–10; Malachi 3:5; cf. Acts 6:1; 1 Timothy 5:16

John 3:14) In our sharing of God's Word, we need to apply Jesus words, "Freely you have received; freely give." – Matthew 10:8, LEB.

We would be remiss if we did not offer a word of caution at the end. Our desire to be selfless does not mean that we must also be foolish or naive. Many of those who are selfish will take advantage of those who are selfless. Therefore, let us be wary of helping such ones. Moreover, women need to be cautious in helping men. For example, they should never give a male hitchhiker a ride. The world is full of evil and our having to end such a positive chapter on a negative note is a reminder of that.

Review Questions

- What is the state of our young people today?

- What can we say of some of young ones ans selflessness?

- What has God instilled in us and why must it be cultivated?

- What motivates us to be selfless?

CHAPTER 4 We Must Love the Truth

2 Thessalonians 2:3-12 Updated American Standard Version (UASV)

[3] Let no one deceive[21] you in any way, for it will not come unless the apostasy[22] comes first, and the man of lawlessness is revealed, the son of destruction, [4] who opposes and exalts himself against every so-called god or object of worship, so that he takes his seat in the temple of God, showing himself as being God. [5] Do you not remember that while I was still with you, I was telling you these things? [6] And now you know the thing restraining him, so that in his time he will be revealed. [7] For the mystery of lawlessness is already at work; but only until the one who is right now acting as a restraint is out of the way. [8] Then the lawless one will be revealed, whom the Lord Jesus will do away with by the spirit of his mouth, and wipe out by the appearance of his presence, [9] but the one whose coming is in accordance with the activity of Satan, with all power and signs and false wonders, [10] and with every unrighteous deception[23] for those who are perishing, because **they did not receive** the love of the truth so as to be saved. [11] For this reason God is sending upon them a working of error[24] so that they will believe the lie, [12] in order that they all may be judged because **they did not** believe the truth but took pleasure in unrighteousness.

Those in the Thessalonica Christian congregation had thought the day of the Lord was already upon them. However, Paul begins chapter 2 by offering them a word of comfort and caution. He says, "Now we request you, brothers, with regard to the presence of our Lord Jesus Christ and our gathering together to him, that you not be quickly shaken from your composure or be disturbed either by a spirit or a word or a letter as if from us, to the effect that the day of the Lord has come." – 2 Thessalonians 2:1-2.

[2:3, 8] *Who is "the man of lawlessness," and what does it mean that the Lord Jesus will do away with him by the spirit of his mouth?*

Many Bible scholars would agree with Knute Larson, who says, "The **man of lawlessness** will be a person so given to sin that he will become the embodiment of it. Here is a man so overcome with evil that no flicker of light can be detected. It is hard to imagine how horrible that will be, especially in light of some of the diabolical figures throughout history which

---

[21] Or *seduce*

[22] Namely, to stand off from the truth, i.e., to not only fall away from the faith, but to then turn on the faith, rebellion.

[23] Lit *seduction*

[24] Or *a deluding influence*

this man will overshadow." (Larson 2000, p. 106) Yes, most believe that the **man of lawlessness** is one person or man, as they believe that the antichrist will be just one person. However, they are mistaken on both counts. The apostle John clearly states there are many antichrists, which is simply anyone, any group, or organization that is against Christ. Similarly, the **man of lawlessness** is a composite man, made up of many individuals from the days of the apostles up unto **the day of the Lord.** Paul said the man of lawlessness was already at work in his day. However, he also says that this lawless one will be destroyed by Jesus on the day of the Lord. (2 Thess. 2:2, 7-8) How could one human live over 2,000 years? The lawless one will be false teachers, false prophets, and atheists, i.e., anyone trying to stand in the way of **the truth.** These ones **stand off from the truth** (i.e., apostasy), to the point that it is a defection, a revolt, a planned, deliberate rebellion. Jesus does away with the composite man [many individual rebels] of lawlessness by **the spirit of his mouth,** which is a figure of speech that evidently represents his commanding call to destroy the wicked in the day of the Lord.

Apostasy Foretold

The apostasy was foretold by Jesus Christ, Paul, and Peter.

Jesus Christ himself warned of this apostasy, in his parable of the wheat and the weeds (Matt. 13:24-30, 34-43), with the wheat picturing those who are truly Christian and an enemy [i.e., Satan] sowed the weeds picturing false Christians. Speaking of the wheat [true Christians] and weeds [false Christians], Jesus said that they are both to grow together until the end of the age, namely, in the day of the Lord. However, when the two are separated, the weeds are burned, that is destroyed. (2 Thess. 1:9) Then, in the book of Acts, we have the apostle Paul warning the Ephesian elders,

Acts 20:28-30 Updated American Standard Version (ASV)

[28] Pay careful attention to yourselves and to all the flock, in which the Holy Spirit has made you overseers, to care for the congregation of God, which he obtained with the blood of his own Son.[25] [29] I know that after my departure fierce wolves will come in among you, not sparing the flock; [30] and from among your own selves men will arise, speaking twisted things, to draw away the disciples after them.

The apostle Paul's words show that the true Christian congregation would be attacked on two fronts. First, false Christians ("weeds") would "come in among" true Christians. Second, "from among your own selves," i.e., true Christians; some would become apostates [stand off from the

---

[25] Lit *with the blood of his Own.*

truth, attack the truth], "speaking twisted things." These apostates will "draw away the disciples [that is, Jesus' disciples] after them," not looking to make their own disciples. The apostle Paul also wrote,

1 Timothy 4:1-3 Updated American Standard Version (UASV) [c. 61-64 C.E.]	2 Timothy 4:2-4 Updated American Standard Version (UASV) [c. 65 C.E.]
[1] But the Spirit explicitly says that in **later times** some will **fall away from the faith,** paying attention to deceitful spirits and doctrines of demons, [2] by means of the hypocrisy of men who speak lies, whose conscience is seared as with a branding iron, [3] men who forbid marriage and command to abstain from foods that God created to be partaken of with thanksgiving by those who have faith and accurately know the truth.	[2] preach the word; be ready in season and out of season; reprove, rebuke, exhort, with complete patience and teaching. [3] For there will be **a time when** they will **not put up with sound teaching,** but in accordance with their own desires, they will **accumulate teachers for themselves** to have their ears tickled,[26] [4] and will **turn away** their ears **from the truth** and will turn aside to myths.

The apostle Peter also spoke of these things about **64 C.E.,** "there will be false teachers among you, who will secretly bring in destructive heresies ... in their greed they will exploit you with false words." (2 Pet. 2:1, 3) These abandoned the faithful words, became false teachers, rising within the Christian congregation, sharing their corrupting influence, intending to hide, disguise, or mislead.

These dire warnings by Jesus and the New Testament Authors had their beginnings in the first century C.E. Yes, they began small, but burst forth on the scene in the second century.

"[Paul says it] Is Already at Work"

About **51 C.E.,** some 18-years after Jesus' death, resurrection and ascension, division was already starting to creep into the faith, "the mystery of lawlessness is already at work." (2 Thess. 2:7) Yes, the power of **the man of lawlessness** was already present, which is the power of Satan, the god of this world (2 Cor. 4:3-4), and his tens of millions of demons, are hard at work behind the scenes.

---

[26] Or *to tell them what they want to hear*

There was even some divisions beginning as early as **49 C.E.**, when the elders wrote a letter to the Gentile believers, saying,

> Since we have heard that some persons have gone out from us and troubled you with words, unsettling your minds, although we gave them no instructions (Ac 15:24)

Here we see that some *within* was being very vocal about their opposition to the direction the faith was heading. Here, it was over whether the Gentiles needed to be circumcised, suggesting that they needed to be obedient to the Mosaic Law. – Acts 15:1, 5.

As the years progressed throughout the first-century, this divisive "talk [would] spread like gangrene." (2 Tim. 2:17, c. **65 C.E.**) About **51 C.E.**, As we already saw above, some in Thessalonica, at worst, going ahead of, or at best, misunderstanding Paul, and wrongly stating by word and a bogus letter "that the day of the Lord has come." (2 Thess. 2:1-2) In Corinth, about **55 C.E.**, "some of [were saying] that there is no resurrection of the dead. (1 Cor. 15:12) About **65 C.E.**, some were "saying that the resurrection has already happened. They [were] upsetting the faith of some." – 2 Timothy 2:16-18.

Throughout the next three decades, no inspired books were written. However, around **96-98 C.E.**, the apostle John pens three letters, wherein he tells us, "**Now** many antichrists have come. Therefore we know that it is the last hour." (1 John 2:18) These are ones, "who denies that Jesus is the Christ" and ones who do not confess "Jesus Christ has come in the flesh is from God." – 1 John 2:22; 4:2-3.

We must keep in mind that the meaning of any given text is what the author meant by the words that he used, as should have been understood by his audience, and had some relevance/meaning for his audience. The rebellion [apostasy] began slowly in the first century and would break forth after the death of the last apostle, i.e., John. Historian, Ariel and Will Durant inform us that by 187 C.E., there were 20 varieties of Christianity, and by 384 C.E., there were 80 varieties of Christianity. Christianity would become one again, a universal religion, i.e., Catholicism. However, that oneness was a false or imitation, as it was by threat of torture and death.

Rebellion Against God

The man of lawlessness places himself in opposition against God, being used as a tool by the great resister- adversary, Satan himself. Paul warns us that this lawless one was/is "coming is in accordance with the activity of Satan." (2 Thess. 2:9) Paul also told the Thessalonians "the mystery of lawlessness is already at work." The identity of the man of lawlessness has be shrouded in mystery, with many scholars supposing it is one evil man, which will appear just before the day of the Lord. However, as was stated above and stated by Paul, the lawless one was already at work in Paul's day. Again, the lawless one is a composite man [many individual rebels], meaning anyone in opposition against God, some worse than others. Some of these lawless ones set themselves up over God by their lying and false teachings, which they place above God's Word, as well as placing themselves in opposition to those who are truly Christian. (See 2Pet. 2:10-13) This lawless one is an imitation, false Christian, who claims that he is truly Christ, "so that he takes his seat in the temple of God, showing himself as being God." – 2 Thessalonians 2:4.

Restraining the Man of Lawlessness

What or who is acting as a **restraint** to the man of lawlessness and the apostasy? It would seem that the apostles of the first century were preventing this great apostasy **from taking hold** while they were alive. In the above, we saw Paul warning that wolf-like men would be infiltrating the congregation after Paul was gone. (Ac 20:29) Paul spoke of the apostasy in many of his writings. In order to keep the congregations clean, Paul taught all over the then known world, taught people like Timothy and Titus, whom he left behind after he was martyred, to teach other qualified men in Paul's place. Paul called "the household of God, which is the church of the living God, a pillar, and buttress of the truth." (1 Tim. 3:15) Paul and the rest of the apostles grew the Christian congregation all over the then known world, going from 120 disciples at Pentecost 33 C.E. to over a million at the beginning of the second century C.E. They wanted to build the purest church possible, **to withstand** centuries of the apostasy that began in full earnest in the second century C.E.

However, the **restraint** of the apostasy and the man of lawlessness (rebels against the truth), were not the apostles alone back in the first century C.E. The restraint of the apostasy and the lawless ones has been those who are truly Christian spread through these last 2,000 years, right up unto the day of the Lord. We have had both men and women who have stood out and stood up for the truth from the time of the martyrdom of Polycarp (69 – 155 C.E.), who had been a student of the apostle John. Keep in mind that throughout the Dark Ages 500 – 1500 C.E., that they may not have taught everything that was biblically true but they were living in a world of spiritual darkness. Catholicism was the dominant influence on Western civilization from late antiquity to the dawn of the modern age (Medieval and Renaissance Periods, 4th – 17th century C.E.). The Catholic Church would like us to forget the good "seeds" of discontent that were present within their midst many years before the Waldenses of the 12th century C.E., 200 years before John Wycliffe (1330-84) and Jan Hus (1369-1415) and 350 years before Martin Luther (1483-1546) and John Calvin (1509-64). (Matt. 13:24) These seeds of men were seeking the truth even in the darkest of periods, even if it meant their life.

Pre-Reformation Seeds of Truth Seekers

- **Bishop Agobard** of Lyons, France (779-840), was against image worship, churches dedicated to saints and church liturgy that was contrary to Scripture.

- **Bishop Claudius** (d. between 827 and 839 C.E.)

- **Archdeacon Bérenger**, or Berengarius, of Tours, France (11th century C.E.), excommunicated as a heretic in 1050

- **Peter of Bruys** (1117-c. 1131), left the church because he disagreed with infant baptism, transubstantiation, prayers for the dead, worship of the cross and the need for church buildings.

- **Henry of Lausanne** (died imprisoned around 1148), spoke out against church liturgy, the corrupt clergy and the religious hierarchy.

- **Peter Waldo** (c. 1140–c. 1218) and the Waldenses, rejected purgatory, Masses for the dead, papal pardons and indulgences, and the worship of Mary and the saints.

- **John Wycliffe** (c. 1330-1384) preached against corruption in the monastic orders, papal taxation, the doctrine of transubstantiation (doctrine that the bread and wine of Communion become, in substance, but not appearance, the body and blood of Jesus Christ at consecration), the confession, and church involvement in temporal affairs.

- **Jan Hus** (c. 1369-1415) preached against the corruption of the Roman Church and stressed the importance of reading the Bible. This swiftly fetched the anger of the hierarchy upon him. In 1403, the church leaders ordered him to stop preaching the antipapal notions of Wycliffe, whose books they had openly burned. Hus, nevertheless, went on to pen some of the most hurtful impeachments against the Church and their practices, such as the sale of indulgences. He was condemned and excommunicated in 1410.

Reformation Seeds of Truth Seekers

- **Girolamo Savonarola** (1452-98) was of the San Marcos monastery in Florence, Italy, spoke out against the corruption in the Church.

- **Martin Luther** (1483-1546) was a monk-scholar, who was also a doctor of theology and a professor of Biblical studies at the University of Wittenberg. Luther disagreed with or argued against papal indulgences, power, purgatory, plenary remission of all penalties of the pope, among many others.

- **Ulrich Zwingli** (1484-1531) was a Catholic priest, who agreed with Luther in many doctrinal areas, in addition to the removal of all vestiges of the Roman Church: images, crucifixes, clerical garb, and even liturgical music. However, he disagreed with Luther's literal interpretation of the Eucharist, or Mass (Communion), as he said it "must be taken figuratively or metaphorically; 'This is my body,' means, 'The bread signifies my body,' or 'is a figure of my body.'" This one issue caused them to part ways.

- **Anabaptists** (i.e., rejected infant baptism, so rebaptized adults, *ana* meaning "again" in Greek), **Mennonites** (Dutch Reformer Menno Simons), and **Hutterites** (Tyrolean Jacob Hutter), felt that the Reformers did not go far enough in rejecting the failings of the Catholic Church.

- **John Calvin** (1509-64) published *Institutes of the Christian Religion*, in which he summarized the ideas of the early church fathers and medieval theologians, as well as those of Luther and Zwingli. His theological views would take too much space. John Calvin had Michael Servetus burned to death as a heretic. Calvin defended his actions in these words: "When the papists are so harsh and violent in defense of their superstitions that they rage cruelly to shed innocent blood, are not Christian magistrates shamed to show themselves less ardent in defense of the sure truth?" Calvin's religious extremism and personal hatred made him unwilling to see and understand the radicalness of his judgments and choked out any Christian principles.

- **William Tyndale** (1494-1536) had to flee from England, published his New Testament in 1526, and completed most of the Old Testament after his betrayal and arrest, in a dungeon. He would be strangled at the stake, and his body was burned. The 1611 King James Version was actually 97 percent Tyndale's translation. He denounced the practice of prayer to saints. He taught justification by faith, the return of Christ, and mortality of the soul.

- Jacobus Arminius (1560-1609), graduated from Holland's Leiden University, after which he spent six years in Switzerland, studying theology under Théodore de Bèze, the successor to Protestant Reformer John Calvin. Rather than support Calvinism, he went against it, especially the doctrine of predestination, which was at the core of Calvinism.

The Darnel[27] Seed of Catholicism

Roman Catholicism has tainted itself with its history of immorality and bloodshed, as well as its pagan-tainted religious ideas and practices. The centuries-long oppression, torture, rape, pillage, and murder of tens of millions of men, women and children cannot come from true Christianity. They were the biggest offenders of the apostasy that Paul said had to come before the day of the Lord.

The Good Seed Protestantism

The Reformation gave us a return to the Bible in the common person's languages, which the Catholic Church had locked up in the dead language of Latin for 500-years. The Reformers brought the common folk freedom from papal authority but also from many erroneous Bible doctrines and dogmas that had gone on for a thousand years. However, the Protestant denominations have found themselves so fragmented and divided; one can only wonder where the truth and the Way are to be found. All 41,000 plus denominations that call themselves Christian cannot be just different roads leading to the same place.

Over eighty percent of Protestant Christianity is liberal-progressive as to their biblical and social beliefs, which began in the late 18th century up until the present. This covers too much area for a summary, but to mention just a few, they treat the Bible as being from man, not inspired and fully inerrant. They prefer to explain away the Bible accounts of miracles as myths, legends, or folk tales. They do not believe in the historicity of Bible characters such as Adam, Eve, and Job. They say that Moses did not write

---

[27] "Darnel, the weed [in Jesus' parable of the Wheat and the Weeds] (species name Lolium temulentum,) is an annual plant that grows in the same areas as wheat. Darnel is nearly indistinguishable from wheat until the ear appears. Wheat ears are heavy and make the entire plant droop downward but darnel's light ears stand up straight. Ripe wheat is light brown but darnel is black. Jesus' parable of the weeds among the wheat in Matt. 13:24-40 builds on the early stage resemblance between darnel and wheat. Hos 10:4, Matt 13:24-40" – (Logos Bible Images by Richard Myers) It should be added that in the roots of these weeds entangle themselves with the wheat, which would make it inadvisable to pull the weed early.

the first five books of the Bible but that they were written by several authors from the tenth to the fifth centuries B.C.E. and were compiled after that. They say Isaiah did not author the book bearing his name in the early eighth century B.C.E., but that two or three authors penned it, centuries later. They claim that Daniel did not write his book in the sixth century B.C.E., but rather it was written in the second-century B.C.E. They claim that the Bible is full of errors, mistakes, and contradictions, as to its history, science, and geography. They claim that the Antichrist is merely good versus evil and is not to be taken literally. Higher criticism has opened Pandora's Box to an overflow of pseudo-scholarly works whose result has been to weaken, challenge and destabilize people's assurance in the trustworthiness of the Bible. Who needs enemies like agnostics and atheists, when we have liberal Bible scholars? We have not even delved into their unbiblical views of social justice, gay marriage, homosexual priests, abortion, women in the pulpits and far more.

Some may ask what about the remaining twenty percent of Christian denominations. Most of those are moderate in beliefs, which cast doubt on the trustworthiness of the Scriptures and give fodder to the liberal-progressive denominations. These are fence-riders, who have abandoned **the Truth** and the Way of true, pure worship within Christianity. Before delving into the so-called conservative parts of Christianity, let us look at the charismatics.

We have charismatic Christianity, the fastest growing segment, which emphasizes the work of the Holy Spirit, spiritual gifts, and modern-day miracles, speaking in tongues[28] and miraculous healing, even fringe groups that perform snake handling in some areas. All of this is <u>un</u>biblical and based on emotionalism.

Those who believe that charismatic Christianity is false Christianity, persons such as this author, are said to be overly critical. Supporters of Charismatic Christianity say we "should be focusing on the fact that while many in the church continue to abandon our Christian faith, the Pentecostal/Charismatic community continues to offer the church a legitimate growth mechanism."[29] I would respond that a denomination founded on, grounded in <u>un</u>biblical beliefs is not true Christianity and are the false teachers and prophets that we were warned were coming by Jesus and the New Testament writers. Therefore, charismatic Christianity is no Christianity at all, and all who are being brought in those groups, are being obscured from finding the path of true Christianity. Further, Catholicism brought in almost the whole world from 400 to 1600 C.E., based on the

---

[28] http://www.christianpublishers.org/speaking-in-tongues-truth

[29] http://tiny.cc/j5d7mx

same false, illogical reasoning from above, this oneness would supposedly be a sign of their being genuine Christianity. However, conservative Protestant denominations would fail to give them a pass.

So-called conservative Christianity is so minuscule that it barely gets press. We should not confuse radical Christianity, such as the Westboro Baptist Church,[30] with truly conservative, fundamentalist Christianity. However, even here within conservative Christianity, we find differences doctrinally, and yes, even in the so-called salvation doctrines.

Are all of the 41,000 different varieties of Christianity just different roads leading to the same place? Are all of the various conservative churches the Truth and the Way? There is no way of knowing for certain, but we know that Christ will bring back the oneness that the first century church experienced before the day of the Lord. We need to return to the question that Jesus asked, "When the Son of Man comes, will he find faith on earth?" (Lu 18:8) Jesus would not find faith on earth at present, not at the level that one might expect, not at present. However, what he would find is many good seeds, those who are truly Christian, who are acting as a restraint against imitation, false Christianity, agnosticism, atheism and every other man of lawlessness.

Believe the Truth

2 Thessalonians 2:9-12 Updated American Standard Version (UASV)

[9] but the one whose coming is in accordance with the activity of Satan, with all power and signs and false wonders, [10] and with every unrighteous deception[31] for those who are perishing, because **they did not receive the love of the truth** so as to be saved. [11] For this reason God is sending upon them a working of error[32] so that they will believe the lie, [12] in order that they all may be judged because **they did not believe the truth** but took pleasure in unrighteousness.

Here Paul is using **truth** (*aletheia*) as something *factual*, a *truth statement* that deals what a fact or reality is. Our eternal future is dependent upon whether we **love the truth**, i.e., what is true. If we do not accept and love the truth, there is no salvation for us. How can we really know whether we love the truth, or that Satan is using unrighteous deception (deluding influence) on us? (2:9) The first question is, "Can we say that we are truly seeking the truth?" Proverbs 23:23 says, "Buy truth, and do not

---

[30] www.godhatesfags.com/

[31] Lit *seduction*

[32] Or *a deluding influence*

sell it." Dave Bland writes, "To **buy the truth** (v. 23) does not mean to pay money for it. Rather it means for one to invest mental, emotional, and spiritual resources in pursuing it." (Bland 2002, p. 213) 'Buying truth' is not as straightforward as one might think. In many cases, it means that we are paying a price; it is coming at a cost to us personally.

What if we discover that a Bible doctrine that is accepted by many denominations is not **the truth**? Suppose that we have spent months, even years, privately poring over this doctrine and find that it is just not biblically true. Do we simply hide that truth and not bring it up, and if it is commented on at a meeting, do we just not participate that day? What if we are reading a verse in the KJV and we decide to compare the ESV, RSV, UASV and the NASB, to find that all of these recent translations read differently than the King James Version? Do we just drop it and ignore that fact because their reading does not support our doctrinal position, a favorite verse in our beloved KJV that we have often used? What if we do investigate and, we find two articles, one that supports the reading in the KJV and one that supports the reading in the newer translations, and we find that the article for the KJV reading seems to be rationalizing and justifying as it really misrepresents the evidence?

Remember, the apostle Paul was known by his Jewish name Saul before he ever met Jesus on the road to Damascus. Young Saul had studied under the renowned Pharisee Gamaliel, one of the greatest Jewish teachers, who may have been there in the area when Jesus was amazing the Jewish religious leaders, at the age of twelve. Gamaliel was the grandson of Hillel, the Elder (110 B.C.E.[33] – 10 C.E.), the founder of one of the two schools within Judaism. Paul describes himself as "circumcised on the eighth day, of the people of Israel, of the tribe of Benjamin, a Hebrew of Hebrews; as to the law, a Pharisee; as to zeal, a persecutor of the church; as to righteousness under the law, blameless." (Phil 3:5-6, ESV) Why was Paul so slow to accept the truth of Christianity, even to the point of his persecuting Christians, and being there when Stephen was stoned to death?

Paul saw Christianity as an apostate, false religion, a break off from Judaism, as it was made up of only Jews before he was converted. Paul had been part of the only true way to God, the Israelite nation, which had existed and received miraculous protection from God for 1,500 years, not to mention the 39 books of the Old Testament. He knew that Deuteronomy said that anyone hung on a tree would be accursed by God. Well, Jesus was executed by being hung on (i.e., nailed to) a wood cross. Paul knew that Daniel and other books said that Jesus would set up a

---

[33] B.C.E. years ran down toward zero, although the Romans had no zero, and C.E. years ran up from zero. (100, 10, 3, 2, 1 ◄B.C.E. | C.E.► 1, 2, 3, 10, and 100)

kingdom that would crush all other kingdoms, and never be brought to ruin. Jesus did no such thing and was executed for treason and as a blasphemer of God. Thus, we can see why Saul/Paul was slow to be receptive to **the truth**.

Nevertheless, Paul did convert. Did Paul buy the truth? Did it cost Paul anything? Yes, Paul had studied under the renowned Gamaliel, meaning he would have been a prominent leader and teacher within Judaism, leading to much wealth. However, in Paul's own words, what did he suffer for the truth? Paul told the Corinthians that he was "in far more labors, in far more imprisonments, beaten times without number, often in danger of death. Five times, I received from the Jews thirty-nine lashes. Three times, I was beaten with rods, once I was stoned; three times I was shipwrecked, a night and a day I have spent in the deep. I have been on frequent journeys, in dangers from rivers, dangers from robbers, dangers from my countrymen, dangers from the Gentiles, dangers in the city, dangers in the wilderness, dangers on the sea, dangers among false brethren; I have been in labor and hardship, through many sleepless nights, in hunger and thirst, often without food, in cold and exposure.[34]" (2 Cor. 11:23-27, NASB; See also 6:4-10; 7:5; 12:7) Sadly, this was in 55 C.E., so Paul had ten more years of even more pain and suffering, before he would be martyred for the truth. So, yes, Paul paid a heavy price for the truth, it cost him much. Yet, concerning such a life as a wealthy, prominent Pharisee, Paul wrote, "But whatever gain I had, I counted as loss for the sake of Christ. Indeed, I count everything as loss because of the surpassing worth of knowing Christ Jesus my Lord. For his sake I have suffered the loss of all things and count them as rubbish, in order that I may gain Christ." – Philippians 3:7-8.

Looking at Saul/Paul, we can establish whether we really have **love for the truth**. Do we have such love for a doctrinal truth that that we will accept it when it is contrary to what we thought was a doctrinal truth? Do we have such real **love for the truth** when a long-held cherished belief is exposed as false?

Imagine the courage that Paul, Barnabas, Timothy, and hundreds of others must have had in the first century Christian congregation. Imagine what is needed today with a liberal-progressive world, Islam being favored over Christianity, many thousands of false Christian denominations that claim to be the truth and the way, with liberal and moderate Bible scholars aiding atheism, not to mention some conservative scholars standing on the line, refusing to take a stand. Again, Paul warned, "the time is coming when people will not endure sound teaching, but having itching ears they will accumulate for themselves teachers to suit their own passions, and will turn

---

[34] i.e., *in cold and nakedness*

away from listening to the truth and wander off into myths."[35] (2 Tim. 4:3-4, ESV) He also warned, "even if our gospel is veiled, it is veiled to those who are perishing. In their case, the god of this world has blinded the minds of the unbelievers, to keep them from seeing the light of the gospel of the glory of Christ, who is the image of God." In the same letter, "And no wonder, for even Satan disguises himself as an angel of light. So it is no surprise if his servants, also, disguise themselves as servants of righteousness. Their end will correspond to their deeds." (2 Cor. 4:3-4; 11:14-15) Many false and imitation Christians prefer to take the path of least resistance, as they possess the spirit of "go along to get along," which means to conform in order to have acceptance and security, i.e., **not** standing up for the love of the truth just to avoid confrontation. Yes, they turn away from the truth of God's Word. Thus, since most are turning away from the truth, do we have the courage of Christ, of Paul, and other faithful ones, to buy the truth, to seek the trust, no matter the cost to us?

In addition, we can tell if we have a **love for the truth** by our heart attitude. The truth should appeal to both our heart and our head. The disciples of Jesus said to each other, "Did not our hearts burn within us while he talked to us on the road while he opened to us the Scriptures?" (Lu 24:32, ESV) It is only when we have true love for the truth; we will follow it no matter where it leads, and regardless of who is on the other side of the truth. If our hearts, like the disciples of Jesus Christ, burn within us, we will be motivated to action, because our salvation is dependent upon whether we really **love the truth.**

Walk in the Truth and Be Taught

Psalm 25:5 Updated American Standard Version (UASV)

---

[35] **4:3 not endure.** This refers to holding up under adversity, and can be translated "tolerate." Paul here warns Timothy that, in the dangerous seasons of this age, many people would become intolerant of the confrontive, demanding preaching of God's Word (1:13, 14; 1 Tim. 1:9, 10; 6:3–5). ... **their own desires . . . itching ears.** Professing Christians and nominal believers in the church follow their own desires and flock to preachers who offer them God's blessings apart from His forgiveness, and His salvation apart from their repentance. They have an itch to be entertained by teachings that will produce pleasant sensations and leave them with good feelings about themselves. Their goal is that men preach "according to their own desires." Under those conditions, people will dictate what men preach, rather than God dictating it by His Word. **4:4 fables.** This refers to false idealogies, viewpoints, and philosophies in various forms that oppose sound doctrine." – MacArthur, John (2005-05-09). *The MacArthur Bible Commentary* (Kindle Locations 60854-60860). Thomas Nelson. Kindle Edition.

⁵ Lead me in **your truth** and teach me,
for you are the God of my salvation;
for you I wait all the day long.

Mounce's *Complete Expository Dictionary of Old & New Testament Words* defines the Hebrew term (ᵉ*met*) "truth" as "faithfulness, reliability, trustworthiness; truth, what conforms to reality in contrast to what is false." (Mounce 2006, 896) Jehovah God, the Creator of heaven and earth, is our only true source of information as to the truth of humanity's current circumstances (i.e., our imperfect condition). He has a complete understanding of everything that he has created, which includes humankind. He knows our design, which means our optimum circumstances for enjoying the life that he gave us. He is also well aware of how to deal with the rebellion of our first parents, Adam and Eve. He is also aware of what the future holds as well.

Psalm 31:5 Updated American Standard Version (UASV)

⁵ Into your hand I commit my spirit;
you have redeemed me, O Jehovah, **God of truth.**

Jesus himself said to the Father in a prayer of the disciples, "Sanctify them in the truth; your word is truth." (John 17:17) Since we are able to place complete trust in every word God has inspired, we need to heed his direction about human behavior, as it is entirely trustworthy. Young Prince Hezekiah says of Jehovah, "all your commandments are true." (Ps. 119:151) The promises that he lays out with his Word the Bible are dependable. After a lifetime of trusting Jehovah, Joshua said, "nothing failed from all the good things that Yahweh promised to the house of Israel; everything came to pass." (Josh. 21:45) Thus, from the books of Moses to the book of Revelation, we see that God is 'righteous and true in all his ways.' – Revelation 15:3.

Walking In the Truth

Adam and Eve were created in the image of God and were a reflection of his qualities and attributes. Even after the fall, in humanities state of imperfection, we still maintain a good measure of that image. For that reason, there is little surprise that the Creator of humankind would expect us to continue to walk in his truth, or that the **lovers of truth** would want to walk in his truth. How are we to accomplish this in our imperfection? The Apostle Paul provided that answer when he wrote, "this is good and acceptable before God our Savior, who wants all people to be saved and to come to an accurate knowledge[36] of the truth." (1 Tim. 2:4) We need to

---

[36] Greek *epignosis*, accurate or full knowledge

acquire an accurate knowledge of who God is, why he created the earth, humans, and his will and purpose for us and the earth. What does he expect of us, his followers? (John 17:3; 1 John 2:3-4) Walking in the truth is far more than mere head knowledge of who, what, where, why and how of things. This knowledge will lead to what Luke called the early Christians, "the Way." (Acts 9:2) This taking in knowledge of the Father and the Son will be life-altering, to the point where it becomes a Way of life.

Certainly, what is true of our human parents would be even more accurate of our heavenly Father as well. God finds great joy, satisfaction, and happiness when imperfect humans choose to imitate his qualities and attributes over their fleshly desires, which lean toward wrongdoing, and over the god of this system of things, Satan the Devil. (Gen. 1:26-27; Pro. 23:24-25) As the Creator and Designer of us, 'he teaches us what is best for us, leads us in the way you should go.' (Isa. 48:17) It is a privilege to work with hundreds of millions of others that want to walk in the truth, to be used in the Great Commission, helping millions more to move from death to life. – Matthew 28:19-20; John 5:24.

We also bring glory to God when we **walk in the truth**. His sovereignty, the rightfulness of his rulership was challenged by Satan, and our choosing to walk with him, means we support him as ruler. (Gen. 3:1-4; Rev. 12:9) Part of Satan's challenge was that created persons would only love him for what they can get out of him, if opposition to their loyalty arises, they will abandon him. (Job 1:6-12) Thus, our continuously, steadfastly walking in the truth, evidence that lie, because we refuse to compromise what is right for some immediate gratification. (Pro. 27:11) For those who have chosen not to walk in the truth, but have followed the path of independence, like Adam and Eve, they unwittingly align themselves with Satan. He is the "father of the lie," "who deceives the whole world," as he is "the god of this age [and] has blinded the minds of the unbelievers." (Jn. 8:44; Rev. 12:9; 2 Cor. 4:4) These have a closed heart and mind and are unable to see the path of truth. May we maintain the mindset of the Psalmist and the prophet Samuel,

Psalm 25:4-5 Updated American Standard Version (UASV)

⁴ ⁴ Make me to know your ways, O Jehovah;
  teach me your paths.
⁵ Lead me in your truth and teach me,
  for you are the God of my salvation;
  for you I wait all the day long.

1 Samuel 12:21 Updated American Standard Version (UASV)

²¹ You must not turn aside, for then you would go after futile things which cannot profit or deliver, because they are futile. ²⁴ Only fear Jehovah, and

serve him faithfully with all your heart, for see what great things he has done for you.

Written for Our Instruction

We can learn some object lessons from what God has disclosed to us in his Word. Paul told the Corinthians "these things happened to those people as an example but are written for our instruction." (1 Cor. 10:11) He also told the congregation in Rome, "For whatever was written beforehand was written for our instruction, in order that through patient endurance and through the encouragement of the scriptures we may have hope." (Rom. 15:4) Israelite history is a great opportunity for us to learn. God personally chose Abraham, Isaac, and Jacob, because they were walking with him while others chose to abandon him. The nation of Israel was the descendants of Jacob's 12 sons.

The Israelites became God's chosen people, of whom he made a covenant, to which they agreed to follow. If they walked in the truth, they would be blessed by God's presence. If they abandoned that walk like the pagan nations, they would lose his presence, resulting in the difficulties that came with living in this fallen world. Whilst they maintained their loyalty, they never became victims to enemy nations. (Deut. 28:7) Furthermore, they could depend on crop growth that was exceptional year after year, as well as their flocks of animals. (Ex. 22:1-15) Additionally, they had no reason to build jails to house criminals, because they had the perfect social system. (Ex. 22:1-15) In addition, they did not suffer from diseases like other nations (Deut. 7:15). Moreover, while they had an army, if they had obeyed, it would have never needed to be used because God fought on their behalf. (2 Ki 19:35)He promised them that they would "be blessed more than all of the peoples," and when they walked in the truth, this proved to be true.

Deuteronomy 7:14 Updated American Standard Version (UASV)

[14] You shall be blessed above all peoples; there will be no male or female barren among you or among your cattle.

We all have the history before us of how Israel just **refused to walk in the truth**. They would walk in the truth for a number of years, and then they would abandon that truth until life was impossibly difficult, moving them to return to the Father. This walking in the truth, abandoning the truth, and repenting to return to the truth, went on for some 1,500 years. The final difficulty in this back and forth was their rejection of the Son of God. His words to them were quite clear:

Matthew 21:43 Updated American Standard Version (UASV)

[43] Therefore I say to you, the kingdom of God will be taken away from you and **given to a nation,**[37] producing the fruit of it.

Matthew 23:37-38 Updated American Standard Version (UASV)

[37] "Jerusalem, Jerusalem, who kills the prophets and stones those who are sent to her! How often I wanted to gather your children together, the way a hen gathers her chicks under her wings, and you were unwilling.

[38] Behold, your house is being left to you desolate!

Just who are **the people or nation** that the Kingdom was to be given to after the Israelites fell out of favor with God? He chose for himself a new spiritual nation, which became the Christian congregation that Jesus established between 29 and 33 C.E. He no longer had the descendants of Abraham, Isaac, and Jacob as his chosen people, by which other nations would bless themselves.

Acts 10:34-35 Updated American Standard Version (UASV)

[34] So Peter opened his mouth and said: "Truly I understand that God shows no partiality, [35] but in every nation anyone who fears[38] him and works righteousness[39] is acceptable to him.

Acts 13:46 Updated American Standard Version (UASV)

[46] And Paul and Barnabas spoke out boldly and said, "It was necessary that the word of God be spoken to you first; since you thrust it aside and judge yourselves unworthy of eternal life, behold, we are turning to the Gentiles.

Did this mean that no Jewish person could be a part of the Kingdom? Hardly! The first disciples of that Kingdom for seven years, 29 C.E. to 36 C.E. were only Jewish people. After 36 C.E., and the baptism of the first Gentile, Cornelius, anyone, including the Jews, could be a part of this Kingdom, as long as they accepted the King, Jesus Christ. Jesus said, "I am the way, and the truth, and the life. No one comes to the Father except through me." (John 14:6) At Jesus' Baptism, there was a voice from heaven saying, "This is my beloved Son, with whom I am well pleased." (Matt.3:16-17) Jesus' teaching, miraculous signs, his ransom sacrifice, and resurrection,

---

[37] Or *people*

[38] This is a reverential fear of displeasing God because of one's great love for him. It is not a dreadful fear.

[39] I.e., *does what is right*

established him as the truth, having the authority and power of the Father.[40] The Christians in the first century were given the position of being God's chosen people. (Acts 1:8; 2:1-4, 43) **The truth** would now flow through Jesus to the Christian congregation. As Paul told the Corinthians, "For to us God has revealed them through the Spirit. For the Spirit searches all things, even the depths of God." (1 Cor. 2:10) It happened just as Jesus had said it would, "I praise you, Father, Lord of heaven and earth, because you have hidden these things from the wise and intelligent, and have revealed them to young children." – Matthew 11:25.

However, more truth was on the horizon with the birth of the Christian congregation. There had been 39 books written by the Jewish writers of the Hebrew Old Testament (2 Tim. 3:16-17), and now there was to be added an additional 27 books by Jewish Christians, making up the Greek New Testament (2 Peter 2:15-16). Thus, there were 66 small books, written over a 1,600-year period that would make one book, which we hold today in our modern-day translations. Yes, some 40 plus Bible writers were, as Peter put it, "men carried along by the Holy Spirit spoke from God." – 2 Peter 1:21.

True and False Disciples

The question that begs to be asked is, 'how do we know, who is walking in the truth and who only appears to be walking in the truth?' Who truly is the dispenser of truth these days? As has been mentioned, we have some 41,000 different denominations that all claim to be Christian, and each would argue that they are doing just that.

Matthew 7:21-23 Updated American Standard Version (UASV)

[21] "Not everyone who says to me, 'Lord, Lord,' will enter the kingdom of heaven, but **the one who does the will of my Father** who is in heaven. [22] On that day many will say to me, 'Lord, Lord, did we not prophesy in your name, and cast out demons in your name, and do many mighty works in your name?' [23] And then I will declare to them, 'I never knew you; depart from me, you who practice lawlessness.'[41]

---

[40] Matt. 15:30-31; 20:28; John 4:34; 5:19, 27, 30; 6:38, 40; 7:16-17; 17:1-2; Acts 2:22

[41] **7:21 Not everyone who says . . . but he who does.** The faith that says but does not do is really barren unbelief (cf. v. 20). Jesus is not suggesting that works merit salvation but that true faith will not fail to produce the fruit of good works. This point is also precisely the point of James 1:22–25; 2:26. 7:22 7:22 **have we not prophesied . . . cast out demons . . .** and done many wonders. Note that far from being totally devoid of works of any kind, these people were claiming to have

46

The primary concern of any true disciple of Christ is that he is **"one who does the will of my Father."** Many times we hear Christians saying, "I think, I feel, I believe," when in reality this is not the right path. We need to establish what the will of the Father is, as opposed to our will, or the will of our pastor, or the will of the people, or the popular will. Maybe we are accomplishing some very good deeds that are done in the name of Christ, but if it is not the will of the Father; then, it is being done in vain. We need to appreciate that the Father has placed all authority into the hands of the Son.

John 17:1-3 Updated American Standard Version (UASV)

¹ Jesus spoke these things; and lifting up his eyes to heaven, He said, "Father, the hour has come; glorify your Son, that the Son may glorify you, ² just as **you have given him authority over all flesh**, so that he may give eternal life to all those whom you have given to him. ³ This is eternal life, that they may know you, the only true God, and the one whom you sent, Jesus Christ.

Matthew 28:18-20 Updated American Standard Version (UASV)

¹⁸ And Jesus came up and spoke to them, saying, "**All authority has been given to me** in heaven and on earth. ¹⁹ Go therefore and **make disciples** of all the nations, baptizing them in the name of the Father and the Son and the Holy Spirit, ²⁰ **teaching them** to observe all that I commanded you; and behold, I am with you always, even to the end of the age."

Matthew 24:14 Updated American Standard Version (UASV)

¹⁴ And this gospel of the kingdom **will be proclaimed in all the inhabited earth**[42] as a testimony to all the nations, and then the end will come.

John 6:38 Updated American Standard Version (UASV)

³⁸ because I have come down from heaven not that I should do my will, but the will of the one who sent me.

---

done some remarkable signs and wonders. In fact, their whole confidence was in these works—further proof that these works, spectacular as they might have appeared, could not have been authentic. No one so bereft of genuine faith could possibly produce true good works. A bad tree cannot bear good fruit (v. 18). **7:23 lawlessness.** All sin is lawlessness (1 John 3:4), i.e., rebellion against the law of God (cf. 13:41). – MacArthur, John (2005-05-09). *The MacArthur Bible Commentary* (Kindle Locations 39114-39118). Thomas Nelson. Kindle Edition.

[42] Or *in the whole world*

John 5:24 Updated American Standard Version (UASV)

[24] Truly, truly, I say to you, whoever hears my word and believes him who sent me has eternal life. He does not come into judgment, but has passed from death to life.

What do we learn from the above texts? **(1)** We need to do the will of the Father, if we are to be walking in the truth. **(2)** The Father gave all authority to the Son. **(3)** The Son, Jesus, does not do his will, but the will of the Father. **(4)** Therefore, to do the will of the Father is to obey the Son, who is doing the will of the Father. Jesus specifically told his disciples before his ascension that he had "all authority in heaven and on earth." Then, he gave them one commission to obey, which was to preach, to teach, and make disciples. In other words, a disciple walking in the truth is one, who is being used as a tool to bring people from all nations over from death into life.

Faithfully Walking in the Truth

3 John 1:4 Updated American Standard Version (UASV)

[4] No greater joy do I have than this, to hear of my children walking in the truth.

The Apostle John penned these words about 96-98 C.E., when he was almost 100 years old. He had spent a lifetime of making disciples, and helping them to maintain their walk in the truth. This writer has spoken many times about the number of denominations today, numbering around 41,000. Those denominations that are walking in the truth today are those that reflect Scripture, as though it were a fingerprint. When a detective lifts a fingerprint from a crime scene, and there is a match to a criminal, it is done by determining how many points within the print match up. We can use this as an analogy for those who are walking in the truth. If we use the Bible as lines in a fingerprint, how many points match up? However, for the sake of argument, let us assume that the reader is in a denomination that highly reflects the Bible, and first century Christianity. How can we be certain that we will be able to maintain our walk in the truth?

There are many difficulties in this life, which can sap us of our strength to continue our walk. Maybe we have grown discouraged because of serious health problems, or family difficulties. Then, there are those that have become distracted chasing after the lifestyles that this world has to offer. What can we do, so as not to drift away, fall away, turn away, refuse, or become sluggish in our walk in the truth?

Consider Jesus Christ

Jesus did not live in an ideal time. He lived under the Roman Empire that expected taxes from its citizen, and he lived under the Jewish system, who demanded their taxes as well. Many Jews were very poor, and the Jewish Law was very oppressive on its people because the religious leaders added so many oral traditions. When Jesus finally started his ministry, he was tempted personally by Satan. In addition, those who chose to follow him were very difficult to deal with, because Jewish pride kept them seeking their own interests. Furthermore, Jesus faced those that mocked him for his message, as well as Jewish religious leaders that were trying to kill him for that message. Moreover, he knew how things were going to end, how he was going to be betrayed by one of the twelve, arrested, beaten within an inch of his life, and executed as a blasphemer. (Matt. 4:8-11; John 6:14, 15) Regardless, of all the difficulties that came his way, Jesus continued walking in the truth. What was it that gave him the ability to persevere?

Hebrews 12:1-2 Updated American Standard Version (UASV)

[1] Therefore, since we have so great a cloud of witnesses surrounding us, let us also lay aside every weight and the sin which so easily entangles us, and let us run with endurance the race that is set before us, [2] fixing our eyes on Jesus, the author and perfecter of faith, who for the joy set before him endured the cross, despising the shame, and has sat down at the right hand of the throne of God.

Paul informs us what it was that enabled Jesus to endure. It was 'the joy set before him." He knew the result of his obedience right up to the very end, and so he kept walking in the truth, as should we. We too can keep in mind the reward of eternal life. (Rev. 22:12) As we are walking through life, there may be, some very atrociously difficult times, where getting up each morning seems overwhelming. If one can focus in on the destination of this journey, it will make each step of the way, just a little easier. Therefore, we can find our walk in the truth, somewhat easier, if we see the life that awaits us.

Consider the Apostle Paul

2 Corinthians 11:23-29 Updated American Standard Version (UASV)

[23] Are they servants of Christ? I reply like a madman, I am more outstandingly one: I have done more work, been imprisoned more often, with countless beatings, and often near deaths. [24] Five times I received 40 strokes less one from the Jews, [25] three times I was beaten with rods, once I was stoned, three times I experienced shipwreck, a night and a day I have

spent in the open sea; 26 in journeys often, in dangers from rivers, in dangers from robbers, in dangers from my own people, in dangers from the nations, in dangers in the city, in dangers in the wilderness, in dangers at sea, in dangers among false brothers, 27 in labor and toil, in sleepless nights often, in hunger and thirst, frequently without food, in cold and lacking clothing.43 28 Besides those things of an external kind, there is what rushes in on me from day to day: the anxiety for all the congregations. 29 Who is weak, and I am not weak? Who is made to stumble, and I am not incensed?44

Philippians 4:11-13 Updated American Standard Version (UASV)

11 Not that I speak from want, for I have learned to be content45 in whatever circumstances I am. 12 I know how to be made lowly, and I know also how to be abounding; in everything and in all things I have learned the secret *of* both being filled and going hungry, both to abound and to be lacking. 13 I can do all things through46 him who strengthens me. 14 Nevertheless, you have done well to share47 *with me* in my affliction.

We have to appreciate the power that is offered to us, just as it was offered to Jesus and Paul, and other servants from the Hebrew Old Testament (Ps. 55:12). It is not the power to fulfill our wishes or desires, but the power to carry out the will and purpose of the Father and the Son. Our ability to walk in the truth through such things as that, which Jesus and Paul walked through, does not come to us naturally. However, this power to endure is very much available to us today as well.

Isaiah 40:29-31 Updated American Standard Version (UASV)

29 He gives power to the tired one,
   and full might to those lacking strength.
30 Youths will tire out and grow weary,
   And young men will stumble and fall;
31 But those hoping in Jehovah will regain power;
   they will soar on wings like eagles;
they will run and not grow weary;
   they will walk and not tire out.

What kinds of things would be in harmony with the will and purposes of God, by which we may be empowered? The world requires so much of

---

43 Lit *and in nakedness*

44 Lit *I am not on fire*

45 Or "*self-sufficient*"

46 Lit *in*

47 Or *have fellowship with*

our strength to cover the necessities of food, housing and clothing. We may be worn out from work, so we need the strength to carry out our daily personal Bible study, going to Christian meetings, Christian activities, and especially our evangelism of the Good News.[48] We may need strength to maintain our Christian walk in the face of temptations, discouragement, or some form of persecution. – Psalm 1:1-3; Romans 10:10; 1 Thessalonians 5:16, 17; Hebrews 10:23-25.

Satan is the god of this wicked age.' (2 Cor. 4:4) Christians are his primary targets, as we are alien residents to his world. Therefore, we should not be at all startled that there is the extra difficulty of living a righteous life in an unrighteous world. When we accept Christ, it is as though we have arrived in a new land, the land of Christianity. It is not an isolated nation but is embedded with a world of nations that are contrary to its very essence of God. It is no easy task to pick up stakes in the land of worldliness. We must let go of old friends, and begin to discover new ones. We must learn a completely new culture. In this land, we are the minority, and most people see us as though we are a stranger in their land. As Christians, our walk in the truth can take us through many difficulties in life, but our destination is living in a renewed world, not this wicked fallen one.

How does this analogy play out for the Christian? We must now learn how to live according to the Spirit, not the flesh, an entirely new moral code. Shortly thereafter, we will develop a new personality that is reflective of our new land of Christianity. "For at that time I will change the speech of the peoples to a pure speech, that all of them may call upon the name of [Jehovah] and serve him with one accord." (Zeph. 3:9) As a new member of Christ's Kingdom, we will have already given up our former ways.

1 Corinthians 6:9-11 Updated American Standard Version (UASV)

[9] Or do you not know that the unrighteous will not inherit the kingdom of God? Do not be deceived; neither fornicators, nor idolaters, nor adulterers, nor men of passive homosexual acts, nor men of active homosexual acts,[49] [10] nor thieves, nor the covetous, nor drunkards, nor revilers, nor swindlers, will inherit the kingdom of God. [11] And such were

---

[48] I am not of the mind of the rest of Christianity, who believe that sharing their conversion, or what God has done in their life is our "evangelism." Our evangelism is to preach the Good News, to teach Bible doctrine, and to make disciples by conversion, much of which is not being done in Christianity at this point and time.

[49] The two Greek terms refer to passive men partners and active men partners in consensual homosexual acts

some of you, but you were washed, you were sanctified, you were justified in the name of the Lord Jesus Christ and by the Spirit of our God.

There are far more benefits to this move from the land of worldliness to the land of Christianity. First, the land of Christianity has a population of persons that live a morally clean life, who accept and love us for who we are, not who we were. (Lu 18:29-30) Second, there is the strength that we are given to cope with this new life, as an alien resident in the land of worldliness. Third, there is God's Word, the Bible, which if followed will generally lead to a far better outcome than the former days of being led by the flesh. Fourth, we now have the hope of life, while before it was the inevitability of death. (Phil. 4:8-9) Most importantly, we will now be a friend of the Creator of heaven and earth. – James 2:23; Matthew 7:13, 14; 1 John 2:15-17

Consider Your Spiritual Health

It is generally true that if we take care of your physical health, we will seldom fall ill; and should we fall ill, the recovery is easier and faster. The same is true of spiritual health. If we fall ill spiritually, the recovery will be easier and faster, if we were healthy to begin with. We need to keep the benefits that we have received from obeying Scripture, and the hope that awaits us at the forefront of our mind. Of course, we cannot completely sidestep the difficulties of this imperfect world or its people, but if we have maintained our spiritual health, they will not overcome us entirely because there is the resurrection hope, which no one can take from us.

Review Questions

- What is the apostasy that was foretold and how long was it to run?
- Who is the man of lawlessness and how will this lawless one be destroyed?
- What rebellion against God has taken place?
- Who has been acting as the restraint against the apostasy and the man of lawlessness from the first century until now?
- What two different types of seeds have grown up together?
- What is the darnel seed of Catholicism?
- What does it mean to believe the truth?
- What does it mean to walk in the truth?
- How can we know if we truly love the truth?

CHAPTER 5 You Must Be like Young Children

Matthew 18:2-3 Updated American Standard Version (UASV)

² So calling to him a child, he put him in the midst of them, ³ and said, "Truly, I say to you, unless you turn and **become like young children**, you will never enter the kingdom of heaven.

Certainly, we would be offended if someone told us, "you are acting like a child!" The irony is, when we think of a child outside of that context, he or she will bring a smile to our face because all children are adorable. However, the comment above is likely relating to their lack of maturity, experience and wisdom. (Job 12:12. *What qualities do children have that adults might want to imitate?*

Developing Childlike Humility

Frequently, Jesus was in "the presence of children around Jesus and/or his love for them is mentioned in the Gospels. See Matt. 14:21; 15:38; 18:3; 19:13, 14 (cf. Mark 10:13, 14; Luke 18:15, 16); 21:15, 16; 23:37 (cf. Luke 13:34). Undoubtedly children felt attracted to Jesus, wanted to be with him. Whenever he wanted a child, there was always one present, ready to do his bidding, to come when he called him. So also here. To speculate who this child was [in 18:2-4] is useless. The point is that this was indeed a child, endowed with all the favorable and amiable qualities generally associated with childhood in any clime and at any time." (Hendriksen 1973, p. 688)

However, on this particular occasion, Jesus wanted to make a point to his disciples and chose a child to do so. Jesus said, said, "Truly, I say to you, unless you turn and **become like young children**, you will never enter the kingdom of heaven." While "adults tend to leave childlike ways behind them (and some such ways certainly ought to be abandoned; children can manifest qualities like pride, selfishness, and temper),[50] but Jesus is pointing out that there are some things to be learned from small children. He seems to be referring to the insignificance and unimportance of children as the ancient world saw them, perhaps also to qualities like trustfulness and dependence.[51] Adults like to assert themselves and to rely on their own

---

[50] Fenton remarks that the child is the symbol of humility "not because a child is humble (most of them are not), but because a child has no status in society." He cites Galatians 4:1.

[51] Melinsky speaks of "unselfregarding trust in God, like that so shatteringly displayed by young children towards their elders."

strength and wisdom. This attitude is impossible for those who wish to enter the kingdom. We should notice further that Jesus does not answer the set terms of the question. He does not concern himself with relative positions and who will have the top job when the kingdom comes: he speaks of the more basic problem of getting into the kingdom. His emphatic double negative rules out the possibility of even entering the kingdom for those seeking great things for themselves. He does not talk about eminence in the kingdom at all; without genuine humility, it is impossible even to get into it, and for humility the question of personal preeminence does not arise." (Morris 1992, p. 460)

Further, "Jesus' response to the disciples showed how selfish and foolish their question was. They were thinking childishly, but Jesus showed them that mature faith is the opposite. Mature faith is childlike humility. In fact, elsewhere in the New Testament, Peter seemed to suggest that the more mature a disciple's faith becomes, the more brotherly kindness and love it demonstrates (2 Pet. 1:5–9). The child Jesus called to him served as an object lesson for the disciples. It was a memorable image to help them learn the nature of true maturity. Little children are the most helpless and powerless members of society. But Jesus infused their childlike qualities with value and greatness. Jesus' **I tell you the truth** might be translated as "Listen up!" In fact, the disciples had not been listening well when he taught the same paradoxical principles in 5:3–12 and 16:24–25. One way to summarize Jesus' first statement is to say that there is a sign on the gates of God's kingdom reading, 'No grown-ups past this point,' or 'No big-shots allowed!' Jesus was not rejecting the positive aspects of adult-hood but the self-sufficiency, pride, sophisticated denial, and self-deception that are learned with years of practice in a sinful world. These negative qualities are not the only reason for God's judgment, but they constitute the "unforgivable sin" of 12:31–32–a stubborn, self-righteous refusal to accept the forgiveness necessary for entry into God's kingdom. At the root of true maturity is simplicity, not sophistication." (Weber 2000, p. 286)

Those who are truly Christian have the heart of a servant, not that of some prominence seeking leader. Those who are truly Christian would have no problem witnessing to a homeless person, with the same love and care we would give to our neighbor or friend. While we do not seek reward, ones with such a heart condition can draw comfort in Jesus words, "Whoever receives one such child in my name receives me, and whoever receives me, receives not me but him who sent me." (Mark 9:37, ESV) When we develop, a generous, humble, childlike heart-attitude, it helps us to draw closer to the Father and the Son. (John 17:20-21; Jam. 4:8; 1 Pet. 5:5) As we learned in a previous chapter, there is more happiness in giving than there is in receiving. (Acts 20:35) Moreover, with a humble spirit, we can contribute to "the unity of the Spirit in the bond of peace" within the congregation. (Eph. 4:1-3) What other childlike qualities might we want to emulate?

Teachable and Trusting

Mark 10:15 Updated American Standard Version (UASV)

[15] Truly I say to you, whoever does not receive the kingdom of God like a child will not enter it at all."

In the above, Jesus brings to our attention another quality that adults can learn from children. While children can be humble, aware of their limitations, because of this, they are also teachable. While older ones do have a more difficult time taking in information, the brain of a child is like a sponge, soaking up information. The question is, "How do children receive gifts? They receive with anticipation. They receive joyfully and thankfully. They receive without believing they did anything to deserve the gift." (Cooper 2000, p. 167)

Thus, if we are to benefit from God's kingdom, we need to 'receive the word of God, which we heard from Matthew, Mark, Luke, John, Paul and the other authors of the Bible, which we accept not as the word of men but as what it really is, the word of God, which is at work in us believers.' (1 Thess. 2:13) 'Like newborn infants, we need to long for the pure spiritual milk, that by it we may grow up into salvation.' (1 Pet. 2:2) What are we to do if we find certain Bible teachings difficult to understand? James wrote, "If any of you lacks wisdom, let him ask God, who gives generously to all without reproach, and it will be given him." (Jam 1:5, ESV) Are we to expect that the Holy Spirit will miraculously place the understanding within our mind if we pray for it, having faith? No, we are to work on behalf of our prayers. Wise King Solomon informs us of how we will find the very knowledge of God. He wrote, "receive my words and treasure up my commandments with you, making your ear attentive to wisdom and inclining your heart to understanding; yes, if you call out for insight and raise your voice for understanding, if you seek it like silver and search for it as for hidden treasures, then you will understand the fear of the Lord and find the knowledge of God. For the Lord gives wisdom; from his mouth come knowledge and understanding." – Proverbs 2:1-6, ESV.

Verses 1-3 shows that it is up to us, as we must search God's words by seeking, "commandments, "wisdom," "understanding," and "insight." If we have watched an old western movie, we know that to search for treasures was no easy task. It called for much digging with a pickaxe and a shovel. The same is true for the Word of God if we are to find "the knowledge of God." We must dig into the Word of God, to discover the gems of truth lying deep beneath word studies, Bible backgrounds,

55

grammar and syntax, historical setting, and the like. We will not find the big nuggets of truth by just skimming the surface of the gold mine.

The Psalmist wrote, "How great are your works, O Lord! Your thoughts are very deep!" (Ps. 92:5) The apostle Paul wrote, "Oh, the depth of the riches and wisdom and knowledge of God! How unsearchable are his judgments and how inscrutable his ways!" (Rom. 11:33) He was not suggesting that it was impossible to discover truths about God, but it will take effort on our part. Paul also wrote, "These things God has revealed to us through the Spirit. For the Spirit searches everything, even the depths of God." (1 Cor. 2:10) Keep in mind that the Bible is inspired (literally, "God-breathed"), and those who penned it was moved along by Holy Spirit. The apostle Peter had this to say about Paul's letters, "As he does in all his letters when he speaks in them of these matters. There are some things in them that are hard to understand, which the ignorant and unstable twist to their own destruction." (2 Pet. 3:15-16) We should be truly grateful for all the study tools that we have which make digging in the Word of God, so much easier.

Babes as to Badness

1 Corinthians 14:20 Updated American Standard Version (UASV)

²⁰ Brothers, do not become young children in your understanding, but be babes as to badness;[52] and become mature in your understanding.

Likely, because of the wicked times we are living in, many children that we see today in movies and on television; they are portrayed as brats. This is shown that way because some there is some truth to it, but these troubled children are reflective of their mother and father's parenting skills. Generally speaking, most young toddlers are unusually pure in heart and mind. Because of this, Paul says we are to be **babes as to badness** (i.e., young children as to badness).

Here "Paul insisted that believers should be as naive as **infants ... in regard to evil**. But Paul did not want believers to be naive about evil. Rather, Christians must be wise as serpents (Matt. 10:16). The ideal is that believers should be inexperienced in and separated from evil, and that they should not know much about it. While he found it appropriate to be innocent regarding evil, Paul insisted that believers should still be **adults ... in** their **thinking**. In other words, with respect to Christian doctrine and practice, Paul wanted the Corinthians to be mature in their perspectives. (Pratt Jr 2000, p. 248)

---

⁵² Or *young children as to badness*

Think of all of the racism in the American news media of late, which has been distorted by older ones. What do I mean? While there are minor pockets of racism in every community of the world, America is not racist as it is portrayed. It is groups like the NAACP and persons such Louis Farrakhan, President Obama, Al Sharpton, and Jesse Jackson, who are race baiters.[53] However, if we drive by and grade school when children are on recess, we will see that they are colorblind. However, in time, many liberal teachers and parents will actually instill racism within the hearts and minds of young black children, having them hold onto something that happened seventy years ago in America. On the other hand, a very small number of white parents will promote racism as well. – Acts 10:34-35.

When we become a Christian, we acquire the mind of Christ and take off our old person, while putting on a whole other person. (1 Cor. 2:16; Col. 3:9-11; Eph. 4:22-24) We are 'transformed by the renewal of our mind, that by testing we may discern what the will of God is, what is good and acceptable and perfect.' (Rom. 12:2) With the help of the Father, Son, and Holy Spirit, along with the Christian congregation, we can remove any stain the world has placed on us while recapturing the beautiful qualities that grew naturally when we were children. – Ephesians 5:1.

Review Questions

- What did Jesus mean at Matthew 18:2-4?

- How can we develop childlike humility?

- How can we be teachable when so much of the Bible is difficult to understand?

- What does it mean to be babes as to badness and what does it not mean?

- What do we acquire when we accept Christ?

- What help do we have in taking off our old personality and putting on the new personality?

---

[53] One who insinuates that racism or bigotry is a dominant factor with regards to an event that either does not involve race or in which diverse cultures are involved are simply a minor element.

Urban Dictionary: race baiter,
http://www.urbandictionary.com/define.php?term=race+baiter (accessed October 15, 2015).

CHAPTER 6 Hearing and Doing the Word

James 1:19-25 Updated American Standard Version (UASV)

[19] Know this, my beloved brothers: let every man be quick to hear, slow to speak, slow to anger; [20] for the anger of man does not achieve the righteousness of God. [21] Therefore, putting aside all filthiness and abundance of wickedness, and receive with meekness the implanted word, which is able to save your souls.[54] [22] But be doers of the word, and not hearers only, deceiving yourselves. [23] For if anyone is a hearer of the word and not a doer, he is like a man who looks intently at his natural face[55] in a mirror.[24] for he looks at himself and goes away, and immediately forgets what sort of man he was. [25] But he that looks into the perfect law, the law of liberty, and abides by it, being no hearer who forgets but a doer of a work, he will be blessed in his doing.

Know this, my beloved brothers (1:19a)[56]

James says **know this,** which is a reference to the fact that these Christians are "a kind of firstfruits of his creatures." '*Knowing* this' is suggestive of action not so much an awareness, which they had. Remember, Jesus said to his disciples that "If you *know* these things, blessed are you if you do them." (John 13:17) A Christian in a righteous standing with God will act on what he knows to be true about God. The apostle John tells us, "No one who abides in him [God] keeps on sinning; no one who keeps on sinning has either seen him or known him." (1 John 3:6) As he has done previously, he calls them **"my beloved brothers,"**[57] (1) to draw their attention to an important point (2), and to let them know that this applies to him as well as them. In essence, James is saying; you *know* that God has made you a *kind of firstfruits* by the *word of truth*, meaning that you should feel privileged, by evidencing your new Christian personality, living up to being a disciple of Christ.

---

[54] Or is able to save *you*

[55] Lit *the face of his birth*

[56] This chapter is from the CPH Christian Living Commentary by Brent A. Calloway

http://www.christianpublishers.org/apps/webstore/products/show/5575711

[57] "**1:19 swift to hear, slow to speak.** Believers are to respond positively to Scripture, and eagerly pursue every opportunity to know God's Word and will better (cf. Ps. 119:11; 2 Tim. 2:15). But at the same time, they should be cautious about becoming preachers or teachers too quickly (see notes on 3:1, 2; cf. Ezek. 3:17; 33:6, 7; 1 Tim. 3:6; 5:22)." – MacArthur, John (2005-05-09). *The MacArthur Bible Commentary* (Kindle Locations 63114-63116). Thomas Nelson. Kindle Edition.

let every man be quick to hear (1:19a)

Just as '*knowing*' in the above was suggestive of an action, so too, "hearing" is suggesting obedience. (John 8:37, 38, 47) In other words, 'to hear is to obey.' Jesus said, "He who has ears to hear, let him hear." (Matt. 11:15) We should not fail to hear aright. It takes more than hearing the audio sound of what is being said, so as to hear with understanding. We are challenged to pay close attention to what the speaker has said and to ask ourselves what he meant by the words that he used. The apostle Paul wrote, "So faith comes from hearing, and hearing through the word of Christ." (Rom. 10:17) What did Paul mean? He meant that by taking in the Word of God, our faith and sureness grow in God, as we see the outworking of his promises. If we are not obeying the Word of God, then, apparently, we have not truly heard the Word of God. We want to move beyond being hearers to being doers as well. All self-importance, willfulness, preconception and personal opinion should be set aside as we humbly hear the Word of God. We should long for the Word of God, seeking it and being eager to obey.[58]

slow to speak (1:19b)

Slow to speak, means that we should ponder what we are going to say. (Prov. 15:28; 16:23) This certainly does not mean that we can never speak. We are to proclaim the Word of God, as we are to contend for the faith and defend the Word of God and to speak the Word without fear. (Matt. 24:14; 28:19-20; 1 Pet 3:15; Jude 1:3, 22-23; Phil. 1:14; 1 Thess. 5:14; Eph. 5:15-16) However, we should not use the Bible as a tool to help others until we have incorporated the Word of God in our lives first. Then we can more clearly see how we might use it to benefit another. (Rom. 2:17-24) Paul speaks to Timothy about those "desiring to be teachers of the law, without understanding either what they are saying or the things about which they make confident assertions." (1 Tim 1:7) We do not want to use God's Word to offer advice counsel, comfort, or even to console until we have first used the Word of God effectively in our lives. The reason for this is simple; the Bible is a book for all those things and more. However, it can be misused in the hands of anyone, who does not have a correct understanding of what it means and has not truly experienced its ability to transform by way of application.

slow to anger; (1:19c)

Injustices surround us in this wicked world, filled with imperfect people, who lean toward sin and are mentally bent toward evil. Yet, James

---

[58] See Matthew 11:15; 13:43; Mark 4:9; 4:23; Luke 14:35; Revelation 2:7, 11; 3:6, and 13.

counsels us to work in harmony with Scripture and prayer to keep our anger under control. Because this is in context with our being obedient to the "word" of God, clearly any analysis of the Word of God must be treated with the correct mindset and heart condition. If we are upset to the point of being angry, he will likely be blinded to the value that lies in the Word of God. (Prov. 19:3) He will not see the light while in a provoked state of mind, let alone be able to apply the counsel in his life in a balanced manner. If another has made us angry by saying something inappropriate or mistreating us in some unjust way, we need to slow down, to avoid responding to them in kind, i.e., some vicious, hostile, spiteful comeback, which will only serve to escalate the anger and the void between us and them. There are times to be angry with righteous indignation, but after that Paul warns us, "Be angry and do not sin; do not let the sun go down on your anger." (Eph. 4:26) This is why we combat the irrational thinking, which contributes to anger, with slowing down and rationalizing the situation before we respond.

for the anger of man does not achieve the righteousness of God (1:20)

No one displaying a wrathful disposition can ever have a righteous standing before God. Wrathful ones will not see the wisdom of obedience to the Scriptures. When angry, we tend to make irrational decisions that will generally not be for the good of anyone, even creating long-lasting ripples within relationships. It could even be as simple as our destroying property in a fit of rage, irrationally not caring about the cost. However, once we are calm, the realization that those seconds of rage have cost us hundreds of dollars if not thousands, maybe even an irreplaceable family heirloom, can be very depressing. Our wrath also makes the righteousness of God difficult to accept by unbelievers who see our fits of rage, as opposed to seeing the qualities of God. If we are always angry, how are we projecting the image of God in giving a witness by our behavior? Can we imagine our stumbling someone out of seeking God because they question God based on our personality? Yes, a wrathful attitude from one who claims to be a Christian blocks the righteousness of God. It will cause the unbeliever to turn away from hearing the Word of God. Solomon writes, "Whoever is slow to anger has great understanding, but he who has a hasty temper exalts folly." – Proverbs 14:29

Therefore, putting aside all filthiness and abundance of wickedness (1:21a)

Here in these passages after James has told these believers the attitudes that they were to have when they come to the Word, he now tells them the behaviors which they must put away in order to be able to accept the word of truth. James tells his audience that they are to be **putting aside all filthiness and abundance of wickedness.** Putting aside carries with it the idea of taking off filthy and dirty clothes and casting them to the side. In other words, they were to take off the old and put it out of the way to be done away with. Keep in mind, while not addressed here, it is important to replace the old with something new. If we do not fill a void, it will return to an unusual extent. If we remove unrighteous anger from our lives, it must be replaced with understanding, compassion, empathy, kindness, and things like these.

For this reason, it is important to note that James is making the point that it is a personal act of the will to do away with these things, and not God's responsibility. The first thing that James tells his readers is that they are to put aside its filthiness. The word for filthiness is *rhuparia* and means "dirty or filthy." (Vine, 1996, pg. 237) Things such as fornication, lust, adultery, immorality, and things like these would be included in the filthiness and wickedness that James is talking about. Also in the context of this verse, James could be specifically referring to the anger of which he just stated does not bring about the righteous life that God desires. The reason James tells them to put aside the filth is because as long as a person lives in filth, it will keep him away from the Word of truth because imperfect humans are naturally drawn to sin. If one is coming to the Word with the wrong attitudes or the wrong behaviors, then he is nullifying that which he is reading or hearing in the Word of truth.

and receive with meekness the implanted word, which is able to save your souls. (1:21b)

After this, James describes the attitude we are to have when coming to the Word, and the behavior changes we must make, he now describes the manner with which we come to the Word of God. We are to **receive with meekness the implanted word, which is able to save your souls.** Meekness is to have a teachable and willing spirit to be ready to submit to the commands that come with the Word of God. It is a condition of the spirit and heart, which means being willing to yield to the commands coming from the word of truth.

Meekness would be the key for these believers to be able to receive, understand, and apply the Word of God into their lives. James states that the Word was already implanted if they would just become humble enough to receive it. James was talking to believers who were living with the indwelling presence of the Holy Spirit. With the inward law being already written upon their heart and the Holy Spirit dwelling within, these believers knew the Word God because it was already implanted. Edward D. Andrews writes about the indwelling of the Holy Spirit,

The Holy Spirit, through the spirit inspired, inerrant Word of God is the motivating factor for our taking off the old person and putting on the new person. (Eph. 4:20-24; Col. 3:8-9) It is also the tool used by God so that we can "be transformed by the renewal of your mind, so that you may approve what is the good and well-pleasing and perfect will of God." – Romans 12:2; See 8:9.

Just how do we **renew our mind**? This is done by taking in an accurate knowledge of Biblical truth, which enables us to meet God's current standards of righteousness. (Titus 1:1) This Bible knowledge, if applied, will enable us to move our mind in a different direction by filling the void after having removed our former sinful practices, and with the principles of God's Word, principles that guide our actions, and especially ones that guide moral behavior.

The Biblical truths that lay in between Genesis 1:1 and Revelation 22:21 will transform our way of thinking, which will in return affect our mood and actions and our inner person. It will be as the apostle Paul said to the Ephesians, We need to "put off your old self, which belongs to your former manner of life and is corrupt through deceitful desires, and to be renewed in the spirit of your minds, and to put on the new self, created after the likeness of God in true righteousness and holiness. . . ." (Ephesians 4:22-24) This force that contributes to our acting or behaving in a certain way for our best interest is internal.[59]

James here is telling his readers the reason they are to accept this Word of God in humility and why they needed to come to it with proper attitude and behavior, i.e., it contained the words of eternal life, it contains the words which places them on the path to salvation. Peter in writing of the power of the word of truth wrote,

1 Peter 1:23 Updated American Standard Version (UASV)

[23] having been born again, not of perishable seed but of imperishable, through the living and enduring word of God.

In the Word of God, these believers learned of the salvation that came through Christ alone. It was the message that they, being wicked sinners at heart, can be saved through the redeeming power of Jesus Christ. This was not just some ordinary book but the very book that leads to salvation and eternal life. It has practical benefits even now, as it will guide us through our daily life and then preserve us for all eternity.

The apostle Paul wrote to the Christians in Rome,

---

[59] http://www.christianpublishers.org/holy-spirit-indwelling

Romans 1:16 Updated American Standard Version (UASV)

¹⁶ For I am not ashamed of the gospel, for it is the power of God for salvation to everyone who believes, to the Jew first and also to the Greek.

Paul also said to the Christians in Corinth,

1 Corinthians 1:18 Updated American Standard Version (UASV)

¹⁸ For the word of the cross is foolishness to those who are perishing, but to us who are being saved it is the power of God.

But be doers of the word, (1:22a)

James is telling his readers to **be doers of the word** as obedience to the Word is not optional, it is required if one is to walk faithfully with God. Jesus pointed out: "Not everyone who says to me, 'Lord, Lord,' will enter the kingdom of heaven, but the one who does the will of my Father who is in heaven." (Matt. 7:21, 24-27) He also said, "Blessed rather are those who hear the word of God and keep it!" (Luke 11:28) The Greek verb (*ginesthe*) is an imperative in the present tense, "be you becoming," which carries the force of an exhortation for continuous action. James is not suggesting they *become* doers, but that they *be* doers, i.e., make sure that they are continuously doers. The expression *doer of the word is* a Hebrew idiom that literally means 'makers of the word.' It could mean a writer or speaker, but more likely carries the meaning of one who lives by the word, one who obeys the word, who practices the word.

and not hearers only, (1:22b)

It does not make one a Christian because they listen dutifully as one is sharing the Word of God. While it is great if a Christian attends Christian services and reads the Scriptures daily, but there is more to being a Christian. Literally hearing the Word, even understanding the Word, is not enough. In the early first century, Jews and Christians had similar services, wherein a lecturer would read from the Scriptures regularly while also explaining what had been read. However, this alone does not lead to faith. If one is to be the type of hearer that James is speaking of here, he would have genuine faith, meaning that his faith in what he heard would result in works. (Rom. 10:17; Jam. 2:20) In other words, a Christian, who was a hearer only, would be one who lacked faith.

deceiving yourselves (1:22c)

Over 41,000 different Christian denominations today are filled with dutiful persons who regularly attend Christian services, regularly read their Bibles, and involve themselves in the social actions of the congregation. In this, they all believe that they are fulfilling their Christian obligations. However, many of these people's lives are no different from the atheist that is a good person, living by the laws, paying his taxes, and doing good to others. We are **deceiving ourselves** if our entire *life* is not inundated in our worship of God. We may not be aware of, or maybe we even block out the fact that obeying the Word of God is an unnegotiable requirement. What we may not realize is that this **deceiving ourselves** is like a roadblock on our path to salvation and harder to set aside than ignorance or skepticism itself. God expects exclusive devotion from his worshipers, which encompasses every aspect of the Christian life. (1 Cor. 10:31) If our worship is merely an outward display, a going through the motions, we are falling short. We were given the great commission of proclaiming and teaching God's Word, as well as making disciples. If we are not regularly engaged in such work in our own communities, we are missing the most important act of obedience.

For if anyone is a hearer of the word and not a doer, he is like a man who looks intently at his natural face in a mirror. (1:23)

When looking into a mirror, man has his image reflected back at himself, where he can see all of his flaws and faults. The purpose of looking into the mirror is so he can see if anything is out of place so that he can make any needed corrections. Can we imagine looking into a mirror, seeing a big stain on our shirt, our hair is completely disheveled, or that we have something on our face, but we ignore them and head off to work?

The image he sees in the mirror is sent to the mind, where it is evaluated, reasoned on, considered. For this reason, by looking at the Word of God, by hearing the Word of God, we are able to see our true selves. We can see all of our imperfections, character flaws, and human weaknesses. We can also see any wrongdoings, misdeeds, even thinking that is out of harmony with the Word of God.

We must keep in mind this analogy is a negative one that is looking at a person who looks **intently at his natural face in the mirror**, sees the things that need to be corrected, but walks away ignoring them. The same is true with the Word of God. He looks into the Word, listens to the needed corrections as he reads, ignores them, and chooses to remain inactive, and fails to respond.

For he looks at himself and goes away, and immediately forgets what sort of man he was. (1:24)

When a person looks into a mirror, he is good at quickly seeing what is out of place as to his appearance. Maybe he has been unable to sleep, so he sees the yellow skin and puffy eyes and dark circles under the eyes. Maybe he sees that he has more gray hair coming in from increased age. When he looks intently into a mirror, he is aware of the things that should give him pause as to how he is living his life. Sleepless nights can cause high blood pressure, heart attacks, strokes, memory loss, diabetes, and lower libidos, and less interest in sex. Does it seem logical to ignore the physical signs of lacking sleep? Should we not consider how we could turn things around? Nevertheless, the man in James' analogy quickly forgets, once he has turned away from the mirror. It is a case of, 'out of sight, out of mind,' as he may want to forget some unwelcome features. Yes, once he has walked away from the mirror he allows the anxieties of the day to crowd out his appearance, forgetting what he may have needed to correct. (See 2 Pet. 1:9) However, the man who is a doer reacts quite differently as he looks into the perfect law.

But he that looks into the perfect law, (1:25a)

James now gives a comparison to the man who not only hears the Word but also actually applies that Word to his life. James says the man who applies the word is he that looks into the perfect law, the law of liberty. The Greek word used for "looks" is the word *parakupto*, which means to "bend inside, lean over, or stoop down to look into." (Vine 1996, Volume 2, Page 378) The sense here is of one seeking to get a better look at something by leaning forward, peering at it. (See John 20:5, 11; 1 Peter 1:12) "The same verb—translated as bent over—pictures the apostle John staring into Jesus' empty tomb (John 20:5). John's look led to an obedient faith (John 20:8)." (Lea 1999, 267)

One, who is wanting to obey the law of Christ does just that, as he peers into the perfect law to inspect, examine and study it, with a heart motivated toward obedience. He is able to visualize himself as it relates to being a biblical father, husband, son, or to herself as a biblical mother, wife or daughter. The law is perfect in the sense that it is complete, everything we in our imperfect state need to walk with God, to have and maintain a righteous standing before the Father and the Son. It is a pathway to salvation through the grace of God. – Proverbs 30:5-6; Psalm 119:105, 140.

the law of liberty, (1:25b)

Jesus said to the Jews who had believed him, "If you abide in my word, you are truly my disciples, and you will know the truth, and the truth will set you free." (John 8:31-32) The Word of God frees his people from slavery to sin and death, putting them on the path of life. (Rom. 7:5-6, 9; 8:2, 4; 2 Cor. 3:6-9) This "law of liberty" is a reference not to the Mosaic Law, but to the new covenant, in which the Father declared, "I will put my law within them, and I will write it on their hearts. And I will be their God, and they shall be my people." (Jer. 31:33) Christians are under the principles of the Mosaic Law, but not under some long code of rules and regulations but rather the inspired, inerrant Word of God, which enables them to know the will of the Father. (Matt. 7:21-23; 1 John 2:15-

17; Gal. 5:1, 13-14) In other words, they have a developed fine-tuned Christian conscience, which leads them in the way that they should go, not because of some fearful dread of displeasing some all-powerful being. The Christian's worship is out of love and is principally positive, not negative. – Matthew 22:37-40; see James 2:12

and abides by it, (1:25c)

James also says that the doer of the word does not just obey it occasionally but **abides in it**. The Greek word for abide is *parameno* which means "to remain by or near" *para*, "beside," hence, "to continue or persevere in anything." (Vine 1996, Volume 2, Page 127) He is abiding by these things in the fact he is daily striving to live these truths out in a manner that is pleasing to his master who gave him these commands. This is moving beyond a mere examination of it. This one is different from the man who had looked into the mirror, being dissatisfied with what he saw, but nonetheless walking away forgetting or even losing interest in what he saw. The Christian perseveres and continues to pore over the perfect law with the mindset of keeping his life in harmony with it. (Ps. 119:9, 16, 97) We need to be immersed and engaged fully with the Word of God, as it guides us through this imperfect age.

being no hearer who forgets but a doer of a work, he will be blessed in his doing. (1:25d)

The Christian, who has moved over from being a forgetful hearer into the world of being a doer, is one who has a biblical mindset. This biblical mindset leads him to every decision he makes, no matter how great or small. Before, he had been one who may have sat listening respectfully but then failed to act on the insights he gained from the Word of God. Now, he takes everything that he hears from the Word to heart (his inner person), the seat of motivation, and puts it to work in his daily life. He now has an inner joy that he had never previously known. The Word of God proves to be beneficial in ways he had never imagined. (Ps. 19:7-11; see 1 Tim. 4:8.) He draws real comfort from the fact that he has a righteous standing before God, and that God finds him pleasing.

Clean and Pure Worship

James 1:26-27 Updated American Standard Version (UASV)

[26] If anyone thinks himself to be religious, and yet does not bridle his tongue but deceives his *own* heart, this man's religion is worthless. [27] Pure and undefiled religion in the sight of *our* God and Father is this: to visit orphans and widows in their distress, *and* to keep oneself unstained by the world.

If any man thinks he is religious (1:26a)

A man may believe that he is religious, i.e., (1) belief in the faith, (2) belief in the teachings of the faith, and (3) living by those teachings in one's daily life. He may believe that he is a devout person, completely dedicated to God. He may be attending Christian meetings, or he may be doing some religious works, which on the surface makes him come across as a genuinely committed worshiper. However, there may be something in his conduct, some flaw, which would cast doubt on the validity of his truly being a religious man. If he is truly, a religious man, his entire life will be in harmony with the Word of God. The Holy Spirit should lead his Christian conscience, the mind of Christ, and inner person by way of the inspired Word of God, not a mere observance of some formalities or ritualistic practices. We need to understand that it is how God perceives us, not how we perceive ourselves. – 1 Corinthians 4:4.

and does not bridle his tongue (1:26b)

James brings to his reader's attention one of the most difficult tasks of the imperfect human, the failure to control the tongue, i.e., what one says, namely bad things. It is of such grave concern that James spends almost all of chapter 2 on this one issue. Not controlling one's speech would include malicious gossip, slanderous talk, badmouthing, impulsive and reckless statements, flattery, using their tongues to deceive, and the like. While he may put on great airs or an appearance of being religious, his tongue (speech) convicts him of being one who pretends.

(1) He pretends to have belief in the faith,

(2) to have belief in the teachings of the faith,

(3) and to be living by those teachings in his daily life but actually behaves otherwise when outside of the churches view.

In James' day, the Pharisees were a self-righteous lot, who used their many words to flatter, to lie, to deceive, and to seek their own glory, while speaking ill of the common Jew as though he were less than human. – Mark 12:38-40; John 7:47-48; compare Romans 3:10-18.

but deceives his heart, (1:26c)

When one begins to think more of himself than he ought, he is surely hip deep in self-deception. Our relationship with the Father and the Son necessitates that we have control over our entire body, which includes the tongue. Paul told the Corinthian congregation that they needed to bring "every thought into captivity to the obedience of Christ." (2 Cor. 10:5) Therefore, if any is living a life that seems to be religious on the surface, yet has not gotten control over the tongue that causes pain to others and to self, this is deception in the heart, i.e., inner person. Even if one has many Christian gifts that stand out, such as being a good speaker, having a warm and charismatic personality, and is generous but falls short in his speech, this is deception. This one has not realized what all is involved in truly being a religious person. (1 Cor. 13:1-3) We cannot practice any sin, and at the same time consider ourselves a genuine Christian. The apostle John makes it clear that Jesus' ransom sacrifice covers the committing of a sin not the practice of sinning, i.e., living in sin. – 1 John 2:1; 3:6, 9-10.

this person's religion is worthless. (1:26d)

First, we should understand that James is not speaking about the religious organization, but rather, the type of worship that this person carries out. This one has a major flaw in his walk with God, his Christian conduct, and so he is not pleasing in the eyes of God who would view his worship (religion) as worthless. This is a case of formalistic worship, not true worship of God, as he has infected his relationship with his self-deception by way of his failure to control his tongue. It is worthless to the point that all he is doing is wearing out the floors of the church as he ritualistically enters and leaves each service. His worship is tainted and polluted and, therefore, pointless or useless.

Pure and undefiled religion before our God and Father is this: to visit orphans and widows in their affliction, (1:27a)

The word that James uses here for "pure" is the Greek word *katharos*, and it means "*clean or unmixed.*" (Vine, 1996, pg. 498) This is the kind of purity that is not mixed with anything nor tainted with anything but clear and clean. It would be like looking at a glass of water from an area that has unclean water, if one swirls the glass, he can see little particles floating around in the bottom, unlike bottled water that is pure and clean. Jesus said in Matthew 5:8, "Blessed are the pure (*katharos*) in heart, for they shall see God." James and Jesus are saying the same thing. In the Bible, "pure" can specify what is clean in a physical sense. However, the word in other contexts can apply to what is uncontaminated, i.e., **not** adulterated, stained or dirty, or corrupted, in a moral and religious sense. Jesus said in Luke 10:27, "You shall love the Lord your God with all your heart and with all your soul and with all your strength and with all your mind, and your neighbor as yourself."

The Greek word for undefiled is *amiantos*, and it means "undefiled, free from contamination." (Vine, 1996, pg. 650) The word carries with it the idea that there is nothing within the inner person of a Christian, which defiles or stains him. Therefore, James is saying that the first criterion is to see if one's worship is pure and undefiled, is in the way that they use their tongue. Then, the second criterion has to do **not** just with the tongue, but also with our actions toward people. Keep in mind, James is not giving an exhaustive list here of what pure worship should be. In other words, there are more requirements than just taking care of widows and orphans and keeping oneself unstained by the world. When listing things, no one ever gives an exhaustive list. It is usually three or four examples, and the inference is *things like these*. The point is pure worship is more than mere formalism, such as following some basic rules, or of attending meetings regularly. Rather, pure worship is that worship, which gets down to the inner person and encompasses his entire life, and which includes his love of God and neighbor. – 1 John 3:18.

James then gives what God would consider being pure and undefiled worship is **to visit orphans and widows in their affliction.** James here is showing that true worship is more than just living by some basic Bible rules and going to Christian meetings, but it involves actions. James mentions two particular groups of people who would have been very significant in his day. He specifically mentions the orphans and the widows who should be of particular interest for those who claim to have pure worship. It is the actions of Christians, who are willing to help those like orphans and widows, who are truly right in God's eye because their actions show forth their true belief. It would have been the orphans and the widows, who would have been the most rejected, and most unlikely to survive the conditions in which they found themselves.

James specifically mentions that these people were to be visited in their times of distress. The word in Greek used here for distress is *thlipsis* and it means "pressure or a pressing together." (Vine, 1996, pg. 17) James is not saying they were to be helped when they had no more troubles, but rather it was *in the midst of* their troubles. They were to be helped as they were going through the pressures of life that were coming against them. This could include clothing, feeding, and give them shelter, and show the love of Christ to them. James echoes what John wrote in I John 3:16-18, "We know love by this, that He laid down His life for us; and we ought to lay down our lives for the brethren. But whoever has the world's goods, and sees his brother in need and closes his heart against him, how does the love of God abide in him? Little children, let us not love with word or with tongue, but in deed and truth." Several Scriptures point to the fact that God has a great concern for the orphans and widows.[60]

and to keep oneself unstained by the world. (1:27b)

This is the third and final criterion, which James presents to Christians to see if their worship is true. The first criterion dealt with their speech, the

---

[60] See Deuteronomy 10:18; 14:28–29; 16:11; 24:17; 26:12; Jeremiah 22:3; Zechariah 7:8–10; Malachi 3:5; cf. Acts 6:1; 1 Timothy 5:16

second dealt with their actions, and now this third test deals with their integrity before God, in the fact that they were **to keep oneself unstained by the world.** The word "unstained" means "spotless" or "without spot." James is saying that the one who is truly religious, pure in worship, will keep himself from being spotted and tainted by the evil and the wickedness of this world. To be stained by the world would be to allow the sinfulness of the world to engage in the evil desires of the flesh. To be stained by the world is to engage in the wicked practices that it has to offer. The word "world" here is a reference to humankind that is alienated from God, who is "lying in the power of the evil one (i.e., Satan)." (1 John 5:19) A Christian should stand out from those using Satan's world fully. (John 17:14) Are we truly separate from the violence and corruption of the world, which would also include our entertainment? Have we adopted any of its attitudes, speech or conduct that would not be in harmony with the will of God? (Matt 7:21-23) Paul warns Timothy,

2 Timothy 2:20-22 Updated American Standard Version (UASV)

20 Now in a large house there are not only gold and silver vessels, but also vessels of wood and of earthenware, and some to honor and some to dishonor. 21 Therefore, if anyone cleanses himself from these things, he will be a vessel for honor, sanctified, useful to the master, prepared for every good work. 22 Now flee from youthful lusts and pursue righteousness, faith, love and peace, with those who call on the Lord from a pure heart.

It is important to note that James says, "keep oneself" from being stained by the world, which signifies that sinning or being polluted by the world is always a personal act of the will. It is the personal responsibility to actively resist the evil desires of the flesh that the world has to offer. Paul said to the Christians in Rome,

Romans 12:1-2 Updated American Standard Version (UASV)

1 Therefore I urge you, brothers, by the mercies of God, to present your bodies a living and holy sacrifice, acceptable to God, which is your reasonable service.[61] 2 And do not be conformed to this world, but be transformed by the renewing of your mind, so that you may prove what the will of God is, that which is good and acceptable[62] and perfect.

The sacrifice that Christians regularly make would be beyond anything that unchristian people would usually consider. Yes, Christians evidence that gratefulness by a life of self-sacrifice. It is toward this that we have made our minds over.

---

[61] Lit *the reasonable (or rational, logical) service of you*

[62] Or *well-pleasing*

Review Question

- [vs 19] What is involved in being quick to hear, slow to speak, and slow to anger?

- [vs 20] How is it that the anger of man does not achieve the righteousness of God?

- [vs 21] Why must we put aside all filthiness and abundance of wickedness? How is the implanted word able to save our souls?

- [vs 22] What does it mean to be doers of the word, and not hearers only, and how would we be deceiving ourselves?

- [vs 23] What does James mean when he speaks of a man who looks intently at his natural face in a mirror?

- [vs 24] What does a man who looks at himself and goes away, and immediately forgets what sort of man he was mean?

- [vs 25] What is the perfect law, the law of liberty?

- [vs 26] How can one's form of worship become worthless?

- [vs 27] Pure and undefiled religion before our God and Father is what?

CHAPTER 7 You Must Be Steadfast and Persevere

Mark 13:13 Updated American Standard Version (UASV)

 ¹³ You will be hated by all because of my name, but the one who **endures to the end**, he will be saved.

The last safe place for Christians was the United States of America with its conservative principles and values and a constitution grounded in Scripture. While the United States is not the Kingdom of God by any means, it has served Christians the world over well and will likely do so right up into the Great Tribulation and Armageddon. However, this is proving to be even less the case, as more and more Christians are coming under fire, taken to court, threatened by a system that has begun to grow more and more liberal by the day. This is because those who are truly Christian give their lives to God's kingdom and will not stand for liberal-progressive morals and values, e.g., same-sex marriage, abortion, the legalization of drugs, weakness on crime, and many other social agendas of the liberalism.

In the above text, Jesus said, "the one who **endures to the end**, he will be saved." What did he mean by endure? The Greek verb behind our English "endure" (*hypomeno*) literally means "to stay under." According to lexicographers is means "**to maintain a belief or course of action in the face of opposition**, *stand one's ground, hold out, endure.*[63] On this Greek verb, William Barclay writes, "It is the spirit which can bear things, not simply with resignation, but with blazing hope . . . It is the quality which keeps a man on his feet with his face to the wind. It is the virtue which can transmute the hardest trial into glory because beyond the pain it sees the goal."[64] Thus, endurance empowers us to stand steadfast and persevere and not lose hope in the face difficulties or hardships. (Rom. 5:3-5) When one is in the midst of pain and suffering, he is able to look beyond to the prize that awaits him. THE BOOK OF JAMES CPH CHRISTIAN LIVING COMMENTARY offers the following on James 1:12a,

> **Blessed is the man who endures under trial; (1:12a)**
>
> James here continues with his progression of the person who is undergoing the difficult trials in stating **blessed is the man who endures under trial**. James calls the believers that endure the trial blessed. The word for blessed is not some joy that the world

---

[63] William Arndt, Frederick W. Danker, and Walter Bauer, *A Greek-English Lexicon of the New Testament and Other Early Christian Literature* (Chicago: University of Chicago Press, 2000), 1039.

[64] William Barclay, *New Testament Words.* 144-5 (Louisville, Westminster Press, 1974)

could offer to man, but rather it was a joy that only God could give to man. It is the highest good possible that only God is able to give man by his own spirit. It is an inward peace and comfort of the soul that is not determined by outward circumstances but is a continuous inner joy through all situations of life. This is the same word that Jesus used to describe the beatitudes in (Matthew 5:3-12).The word for **endures** is *hupomone* that means to "*remain under.*" (Vine, 1996, pg. 200) The blessedness that James talks about only comes to the one who remains firm in his faith in the midst of the trial. (Calloway 2015, p. 22)

Hebrews 12:1 Updated American Standard Version (UASV)

[1] Therefore, since we have so great a cloud of witnesses surrounding us, let us also **lay aside every weight** and the sin which so easily entangles us, and **let us run with** endurance (*hypomones*) the race that is set before us,

One would not argue that the times we now live in are truly difficult, as they are violent in the extreme, designed to cater to our fleshly side, and both parents must work just to get by. All of this is by design, to cause Christians to take their eye off the one assignment that Jesus gave us. (Matt 24:14; 28:19-20; Ac 1:8) The words of the apostle Paul in the book of Hebrews is ever applicable to us as well, as we too need to **lay aside every weight, and sin which clings so closely, run with** endurance **the race that is set before us.**

"Lay aside every weight" is a reference to the Greek and Roman athletic games. "In the context of running, it could refer to burdensome clothing or excess body weight. Therefore, believers are to run the Christian race with **endurance**, laying aside those things that bind or weigh us down."[65] What type of weight could hinder us in the race that is set before us? We would want to set aside any constant thinking about a particular matter or persistent interest, such as fame or making as a reputation for ourselves, love of money, sexual immorality or violent entertainment, excessive travel for pleasure,[66] and other material pursuits that can affect our thinking. – 1 John 2:15-17.

---

[65] Clinton E. Arnold, Zondervan Illustrated Bible Backgrounds Commentary Volume 4: Hebrews to Revelation., 75 (Grand Rapids, MI: Zondervan, 2002).

[66] There is nothing wrong with traveling more when you are retired, or even taking a vacation once or twice a year with your family up unto the time of retirement. However, the key word is "excessive." If John Smith truly believed that he was going to receive everlasting life; then, this life should be used to almost entirely to carry out the work Christians were given (Matt 28:19-20). Let us play with the belief and reality of everlasting life. The 70-80 years that we now live is

Constant thinking about or persistent interest, however, can wear us out emotionally, physically, and spiritually, affecting our trust in God. Paul talks about how a lack of faith is **"sin which clings so closely."** Imperfect humans, even Christians with the new personality and mind of Christ, have a propensity at finding themselves in periods of temporary weakness of faith. In these moments, they tend to act contrary to the Spirit's lead, through deception, human weaknesses, setting their hearts on other things, which in turn grieves the Holy Spirit, ending with their stumbling spiritually. Endurance empowers one to be steadfast if the face of hurdles and adversities all the while maintaining hope.

Pay Much Closer Attention

Hebrews 2:1 Updated American Standard Version (UASV)

² For this reason we must pay much closer attention to the things that have been heard, so that we do not drift away from it.

What and where was the very first Christian congregation? It was the Jerusalem Christian congregation, founded right after Pentecost of 33 C.E. It was made up of the 12 apostles, Jesus brothers James and Jude, Mark who wrote the Gospel that bears his name, and hundreds of other Jews that personally knew Jesus, many traveling with him. We can only imagine how spiritually strong that congregation must have been. (Acts 2:44-47; 4:32-34; 5:41; 6:7) However, some 31 years later in 61-64 C.E., the congregation had grown tired and apathetic. Some were drifting away (2:1), others were falling away (6:6) or willfully begging off or turning away (12:25), while other had become sluggish (6:12) and some were shrinking back (10:39) from the truth that they had known from the beginning. How could this have happened? One resource writes,

> The persons addressed were in the mental and spiritual condition common in every age of the Christian church, a condition of languor [laziness] and weariness, of disappointed expectations, deferred hopes, conscious failure and practical unbelief. They were Christians but had slender appreciation of

---

what, when we think of say several hundred billion trillion years that lies ahead in our everlasting life. If a true believer saw it that way, this Great Commission of preaching, teaching, and making disciples would be taken more seriously. Here is how we should view pleasure and entertainment, as a means to recuperate, before getting back to our Great Commission. The commission is called great for a reason, and the analogy I gave for John smith, is like one piece of sand, in comparison to all of the sand on all of the planets in the 125 billion universes. That piece of sand, our 70-80 years of life now is not even on the scale of significance. My comment was for the wealthy Christian family, who travels for pleasure, **excessively**.

the glory of their calling, misconstrued their experience, and had allowed themselves to drift away from boldness and hope and intensity of faith.[67]

The comment from above, "the mental and spiritual condition common in every age of the Christian church," is the reason, we are going to review what the author of Hebrews wrote, to pull that first Christian congregation out of their spiritual stupor. The first seven years of Christianity, from 29 C.E., when the founder Jesus Christ was baptized, to 36 C.E., when the first Gentile was baptized, the Christian congregation was made up of Jews only. Some of these ones were very slow in getting over that there was a new way to God, through Jesus Christ. It was deeply embedded in their mind and heart that the only way to God for 1,500 years was through the Israelite nation, and the Mosaic Law. The system of worship that they had known throughout their entire life was now replaced with a new one. They had, under the old Jewish system, an extraordinary system of worship, priesthood, regular sacrifices, and a temple in Jerusalem that could be viewed as the ninth wonder of the world. Many Jewish Christians were unable to make the transition, as they walked aimlessly because of an inability to see how the Christian system was better than the Jewish system of the past, failing to get in the race for life.

Romans 10:4 Updated American Standard Version (UASV)

[4] For Christ is the end of the law for righteousness to everyone who believes.

On Romans 10:4, Kenneth Boa and William Kruidenier, write, "As the **end of the law**. Christ made it possible for **everyone who believes** to attain a righteous standing before God. As the **end** (*telos*) **of the law**. Christ was its fulfillment (Matt. 5:17; Rom. 10:4), not its chronological termination (Rom. 6:15). However, it was his fulfillment of the law's requirements, and his resulting confirmation in righteousness, that cast the law aside as a tormentor of all who bore the guilt of not keeping it."[68]

What about today, with Christians coming out of the world into the Christian congregation, is it not similar? The world is full of wonderment, powerful leaders, exciting innovations, scientific advancements, stimulating opportunities, and it is specifically designed to lure the unsuspecting one into its ways of thinking, and to retain them once they have them, as well

---

[67] W. Robertson Nicoll, The Expositor's Greek New Testament, Volume Four, 236 (Peabody: Hendrickson, 2002).

[68] Kenneth Boa and William Kruidenier, *Romans*, vol. 6, Holman New Testament Commentary (Nashville, TN: Broadman & Holman Publishers, 2000), 309.

as pull them back in if they ever choose to leave. It has generated a generation of **selfish, me-first people** that set aside God's Word, because they develop a wall of disbelief, setting impossible standards for the Bible while lowering the standards of secularism,[69] which enables them to feel good about being in the world or returning to the world. Then, there are the Christians who are **halfhearted,** having little enthusiasm, interest, support, or conviction in their worship of God. – Psalm 119:113; Revelation 3:16.

Finally, there are those, who possess **"a double heart"** (Literally "a heart and a heart").[70] (Ps 12:2) In other words, these ones, go to every congregation meeting, are very active in their congregation, and at the same time, they are living a very worldly life outside of the congregation. It might be that they are materialistic, or they are morally unclean (1 Pet 2:12; He 4:13; 1 Cor. 6:9-11), mentally unclean (Phil 4:8; Matt 15:18-20), unclean in speech (Eph. 4:25, 29, 31; 5:3; Rev 21:8), and so on. They may lie, gamble, or steal by cheating on their taxes, or dishonest business practices. (Pro 6:16-19; Cols 3:9, 10) They may have fits of anger and are abusive to their wife, or children. (Ps 11:5; Proverbs 22:24, 25) They may be heavy drinkers and drunkards, which leads to their household problems. (1 Cor. 5:11-13; 1 Tim. 3:8) These ones are those who are deceptively presenting themselves as one thing to the Christian congregation while living an entirely different life outside of the congregation. – Matthew 15:7-8.

So again, we revisit Paul's words to this Jewish congregation, **"Therefore,** we must **pay much closer attention** to what we have heard, lest we **drift away** from it." (Heb. 2:1)

Therefore is an adverb that introduces a statement that is a consequence of the previous statement. Chapter 1 of Hebrews was/is about the supremacy of God's Son. Chapter 3 is similarly about Jesus being greater than Moses is while chapter 4 demonstrates that Jesus is a superior high priest than in the Aaronic priesthood, and chapters 5 through 7 cover the superiority of Jesus to Melchizedek.[71] Thus, the "therefore," that begins chapter 2 is expressing that there is a serious need to consider the greatness of Christ, and to learn more about Jesus. However, they needed to **pay much closer attention** to what we have heard, better appreciating the

---

[69] Secularism is the rejection of religion or its exclusion from a philosophical or moral system.

[70] Footnote, Lexham English Bible

[71] A priest and king of Salem who blessed Abraham, and in essence, blessed the Aaronic priesthood that was in his loins.

superiority of Jesus, and to negate the impressive Jewish system that had been their way for so long.

The idea of **drifting away** was a reference to ship sailing, which was a common mode of transportation in the first-century C.E. Roman Empire. If the captain of a ship does not keep his mind on the wind and current, he will risk running his ship past a safe harbor and onto rocky seashore. These Jewish Christians needed to pull themselves out of their apathetic stupor. In the same way, if we are not heeding the Word of God, by way of a regular, deep personal Bible study, preparing for our Christians meetings, so as to participate, sharing our faith with others, we too will drift ashore, experiencing spiritual shipwreck. Sadly, some shipwrecks are beyond recovery, and some crashes of one's faith place them beyond repentance. In other words, nothing will ever move them to repent. Just like a captain, who is not paying attention, we may not wake up until it is too late. Thus, let us catch any spiritual stupor before it becomes serious.

An Evil and Unbelieving Heart

Hebrews 3:12-13 Updated American Standard Version (UASV)

[12] Take care, brothers, lest there be in any of you an evil, **heart of unbelief**, leading you to **fall away** from the living God. [13] But exhort one another every day, as long as it is called "today," that none of you may be **hardened** by the deceitfulness of sin.

We cannot remain "pure in heart" (Matt 5:8), if we develop an evil **heart of unbelief**. An evil heart of unbelief (*kardia ponera apistias*) is "a remarkable combination. Heart ([kardia]) is common in the LXX[72] (about 1,000 times), but "evil heart" only twice in the O.T. (Jer. 16:12; 18:12). "[*Apistias*] is more than mere unbelief, here rather disbelief, refusal to believe, genitive case describing the evil heart marked by disbelief which is no mark of intelligence then or now."[73]

What beliefs have the world of mankind spread that would undermine one's faith in God to such an extent? **(1) Evolution** is the theoretical process by which all species develop from earlier forms of life. **(2) Relativism** is the belief that concepts such as right and wrong, goodness and badness, or truth and falsehood are not absolute but change from culture to culture and situation to situation. **(3) Limited inerrancy** as oppose to full inerrancy has

---

[72] LXX is the Greek Septuagint, a Greek translation of the Hebrew Bible made between 280 to 150 B.C.E. to meet the needs of Greek-speaking Jews outside Palestine.

[73] A.T. Robertson, Word Pictures in the New Testament, Heb 3:12 (Nashville, TN: Broadman Press, 1933).

caused many to lose their faith. Full inerrancy affirms that the original Scriptures contained no errors at all. Limited inerrancy, on the other hand, affirms that Scripture is without error in matters of salvation doctrine, but not history, science, or geography. **(4) Secularism** is the rejection of religion or its exclusion from a philosophical or moral system. **(5) Atheism** is disbelief in the existence of God or deities. **(6) Biblical criticism** is known as the historical-critical method of Bible study, such as the study of historical criticism, literary criticism, form criticism, tradition criticism, redaction criticism, structuralist criticism, among others. This is known as the new way of biblical interpretation, and it undermines the trustworthiness of Scripture, a pseudo-scholarship. **(7) Empiricism** is the philosophical belief that all knowledge is derived from the experience of the senses, to the exclusion of revelatory knowledge, such as the Word of God. **(8) Existentialism** is a philosophical movement begun in the 19th century that denies that the universe has any intrinsic meaning or purpose. It requires people to take responsibility for their own actions and shape their own destinies. **(9) Pragmatism** is the position that "those beliefs are true which it is expedient for us to act upon and believe." **(10) Religious Liberalism** is a movement in Protestantism stressing intellectual freedom and the moral content of Christianity over the doctrines of traditional theology. The abandonment of "the traditional view of authority and truth in order to substitute a newer source of authority, typically based on experience or intellectual conclusions."[74] This list could go on for some time, but I believe you have gotten the point. The Word of God, true Christianity, and truth has been under an ever-greater attack throughout the 20th and into the 21st century, the pinnacle of the enlightenment age that got its start in the late 17th century with René Descartes. We must not let ourselves be caught off guard by such death-dealing beliefs.

What is the result of an unbelieving heart that has been infected with the thinking of man? It leads one to **fall away** (Gr., *apostenai,* "to stand off") from the living God. Just how serious is this? You will notice that earlier, Paul spoke of '**drifting away**' because of not paying attention to one's spiritual needs. (Heb. 2:1; Matt 5:3) However, the Greek term *apostenai* rendered "fall away," which is more of a willful drawing away, means "to stand off" and is related to the word "apostasy." This is standing off from the truth that was once accepted. It signifies a willful and purposeful resisting, withdrawing, and abandoning, with a measure of disdain added. One New Testament word study book offered,

> The word "departing" deserves special attention. It is *aphistemi* which is made up of *apo* "off," and *histemi* "to stand,"

---

[74] Hindson, Ed (2008-05-01). The Popular Encyclopedia of Apologetics (Kindle Locations 11777-11778). Harvest House Publishers. Kindle Edition.

the compound word meaning "to stand off from." This was exactly the position of these Hebrews. They were standing aloof from the living God. The idea is not that of departing, but of standing off from. Our word "apostasy" is derived from a form of this Greek word. Apostasy is defined as the act of someone who has previously subscribed to a certain belief, and who now renounces his former professed belief in favor of some other, which is diametrically opposed to what he believed before. In other words, his new belief is not merely a new system of faith, but one, which at every point negates his former belief.[75]

As was stated, the **drifting away** of Hebrews 2:1 is the result of being inattentive to one's spiritual needs, and bears repeating. In that circumstance, there is no real effort involved to end up spiritually shipwrecked. However, this **falling away** is the result of someone taking action. This one is willfully "falling away from the living God." Why? Paul gives us the answer, an evil, **heart of unbelief.** This evil heart of unbelief is **not** the result of not being a student of the Bible, nor having sufficient knowledge of Scripture, or even an incorrect understanding of Scripture. Paul goes on to quote the occasion of the Israelites at Exodus 15, which is also referenced at Psalm 95:8, "do not harden your hearts as in the rebellion" at Meribah. The Israelites had enjoyed Jehovah's God's love, protection, and saw his "works for forty years" while in the wilderness. (Heb. 3:7-11) However, these very ones hardened their hearts against him.

In the same sense, Christians today, need to "consider how to stir up one another to love and good works, not neglecting to meet together, as is the habit of some, but encouraging one another" (Heb. 10:24-25), so that "none of you may be **hardened** by the deceitfulness of sin." What we have learned thus far? **(1)** We do not want to neglect personal Bible study. **(2)** We should be well prepared for congregation meetings **(3)** We should have mercy on those who have begun to doubt because they have fed their minds on literature from Bible critics; and we should have the ability to reason from the Scriptures, to help them overcome their doubts. **(4)** In addition, we stir up one another to love and good works, not neglecting to meet together. – Hebrews 10:24-25.

Am I suggesting that Christians should never read a book by a Bible critic? No. However, would you venture into any unsafe place in life without preparing for it first? Let me offer an illustration. A prosecuting attorney goes to the best law school in the US, studies under one of the greatest legal minds, and he may have 30-years of experience. He puts on

---

[75] Kenneth S. Wuest, Wuest's Word Studies from the Greek New Testament: For the English Reader, Heb 3:12 (Grand Rapids: Eerdmans, 1997).

the state's case, we are mesmerized by his knowledge of the law, the skill with which he presents it, and we find the defendant guilty as we sit in the jury box. However, one thing is missing. What? We have yet to hear the defense attorney. Do we now have blinders to the point that it does not matter? The irony is, once the defense attorney gets up and presents his case, we are so stunned by the evidence that he presents, that we have now completely changed our position.

This is what would happen if we read the Bible critics book first. We would feel that it really cast doubts about the existence of a personal God, who created everything, and that such a being inspires the Bible is no longer true. Then, we read an apologetic Bible scholar's book that deals with the same issues say that of Dr. William Lane Craig, concluding we did not have all the facts, and now feel saddened because we doubted in the first place. What I recommend is that we read the apologetic Bible scholar's book first, like putting in a bulletproof vest, and then read the Bible critic's book if we so desire.

Do Not Shrink Back to Destruction

Hebrews 10:39 Updated American Standard Version (UASV)

[39] But we are not of those who **shrink back** to destruction, but of those who have faith to the preserving of the soul.

Paul closes this section with serious confidence that they "are not of those who **shrink back** and are destroyed." Today, true Christians live in a time like no other, and are under a constant bombardment from the world that surrounds us. Like Paul and the Jewish Christians, who heeded his counsel, we too do not want to shrink back to destruction. This does not mean that we will never have a moment of fear, as we are susceptible to being afraid like any other imperfect human. The Greek *hupostello*, means "'to draw back, withdraw,' perhaps a metaphor from lowering a sail and so slackening the course, and hence of being remiss in holding the truth."[76] A Christian with faith, will not 'drawback or withdraw' from their commitment to God's will and purposes, 'slacking off in their course.' Regardless of what this wicked world, alienated from God throws at them, such as persecution, difficulties, health issues, or any other tribulation. They will face these head-on, like the apostle Paul, who said, "For the sake of Christ, then, I am content with weaknesses, insults, hardships, persecutions, and calamities. For when I am weak, then I am strong." (2 Cor. 12:10) Yes,

---

[76] W. E. Vine, Merrill F. Unger and William White, Jr., vol. 2, Vine's Complete Expository Dictionary of Old and New Testament Words, 180 (Nashville, TN: T. Nelson, 1996).

we must be steadfast in our service to God, as he is well aware of our limitations, and he makes allowances for these, "he remembers that we are dust."—Psalm 55:22; 103:14.

Do Not Grow Weary or Fainthearted

Hebrews 12:3 Updated American Standard Version (UASV)

³ For consider the one who endured such hostility by sinners against himself, so that you will not **grow weary** in your souls and give up.

What is it that we are not to grow weary or fainthearted from? What is it Satan would love us to get too tired to carry out? The answer is found in verses 1-2.

Hebrews 12:1-2 Updated American Standard Version (UASV)

¹ Therefore, since we have so great a cloud of witnesses surrounding us, let us also lay aside every weight and the sin which so easily entangles us, and let us **run with endurance the race** that is set before us, ² **fixing our eyes on Jesus**, the author, and perfecter of faith, who for the joy set before Him endured the cross, despising the shame, and has sat down at the right hand of the throne of God.

Have you bought out the time to know why Jesus ever came to earth as a man in the first place? First, we can say that the Gospels are of his life and ministry. From this, you can see that his focus was on his ministry. Jesus came to earth as a man for three reasons. **(1)** Jesus said, "For this purpose, I was born and for this purpose I have come into the world—to bear witness to the truth." (John 18:37) **(2)** Peter said this to Christians, "For to this you have been called, because Christ also suffered for you, leaving you an example, so that you might follow in his steps." (1 Pet. 2:21) **(3)** Jesus tells us this, "even as the Son of Man came not to be served but to serve, and to give his life as a ransom for many." (Matt. 20:28) Jesus came to leave us an example, for us to follow in his steps, which example is his ministry that he carried out to the Jews of his day, and we are to carry out to all people. (Matt. 28:19-20) The sad irony, there are really no churches within the 39,000 denominations that I am aware of based on my personal statistical surveys, which have even begun to carry out a similar message to the nations, so there is no real reason to be tired out from this work. Oh yes, they send out missionaries here and there, but the truth is, **all Christians** are responsible for preaching, teaching and making disciples. With or without the church, we need to make progress toward maturity and improve our ministry (evangelistic) skills, so as to carry out the Great Commission we were given.

Review Questions

- Jesus said, "The one who **endures to the end**, he will be saved." What did he mean by endure?

- Why is it paramount that Christians have endurance?

- Explain what Paul meant by "pay much closer attention to the things that have been heard."

- How can Christians develop an evil, unbelieving heart?

- How can Christians shrink back to destruction?

- How can Christians grow weary and fainthearted?

CHAPTER 8 You Must Walk in the Light

1 John 1:5-7 Updated American Standard Version (UASV)

⁵ This is the message we have heard from him and proclaim to you, that God is light, and there is no darkness at all in him. ⁶ If we say we have fellowship with him and yet we are **walking in the darkness,** we are lying and are not practicing the truth; ⁷ but if **we are walking in the light,** as he is in the light, we have fellowship with one another, and the blood of Jesus his Son cleanses us from all sin.

First, it should be noted that John's statement that "the blood of Jesus his Son cleanses us from all sin," does not mean that we are able to go without sinning, or that our sinful nature is miraculously removed. Rather, John meant that the blood of Jesus cleanses from "every kind of sin and shows there is no limit to the categories of sin that Christ is willing to forgive. His sacrificial death made every type of sin forgivable." (Larson 2000, p. 158)

The ultimate Source of life (genuine and ultimate life, i.e., eternal life.) is the Father, who has 'given all authority in heaven and on earth to the Son.' (Matt. 28:20) Therefore, Jesus is the source of eternal life to humans as well. The prophet Daniel foretold that 'Jesus would be given authority to rule, and glory, and a kingdom; so that those of every people, nation, and language should serve him.' (Dan. 9:7) Jesus himself specifically said, "All things have been handed over to me by my Father." (Matt. 11:27, ESV) On another occasion, Jesus said, "The Father loves the Son and has given all things into his hand." (John 3:35, ESV) Paul wrote, "For "he [God] subjected all things under his [Jesus'] feet." But when it says "all things" are subjected, it is clear that the one [God] who subjected all things to him [Jesus] is not included." Our point is made by Jesus prayerful words to the Father in John 17:1-3 (ESV), "**Father,** the hour has come; **glorify your Son** that the Son may glorify you, since you have **given him authority over all** flesh, **to give eternal life** to all **whom you have given** him. And this is eternal life, that they know you the only true God, and Jesus Christ whom you have sent." Thus, the Father has given all authority in heaven and on earth to the Son, to give eternal life to all that the Father had placed in his hands. Thus, Jesus is the source of eternal life by way of the Father giving him all authority.

Passed from Death to Life

John **5:24** Updated American Standard Version (ASV)

²⁴ Truly, truly, I say to you, whoever hears my word and

1 John **3:14** Updated American Standard Version (UASV)

¹⁴ We know that we have **passed over from death to life** because we love

believes him who sent me has eternal life. He does not come into judgment, but has **passed from death to life.**

the brothers. The one who does not love remains in death.

Here at John 5:24, Jesus is speaking about those who are truly Christian. These ones were once spiritually dead. However, upon hearing Jesus' words and having faith in him, these ones are no longer walking in the darkness (practicing sin). They 'passed from death to life' in that their being condemned to death has been removed from them, and they are given the hope of eternal life because of their faith in Jesus Christ.

Commenting on 1 John 3:14, David Walls and Max Anders say, "True Christians, those born of God, have love for their brothers placed in their hearts by the Lord, so that we **know that we have passed from death to life, because we love our brothers.** Loving our brothers does not give us eternal life. God does that through Christ. If we have eternal life, we will manifest it by loving our brothers. We may have difficulty loving some Christians who make it hard to love them, but a fundamental desire to love them will show through our lives. Even Jesus' disciples quarreled among themselves about who would be the greatest among them. That was an unloving thing to do. It did not, however, relegate them to the realm of the unsaved." (Walls and Anders 1996, p. 197)

Those who are truly Christian are grateful for the Father, the Source of genuine and ultimate life, namely, eternal life, as well as his having 'given the Son all authority in heaven and on earth to the Son.' What does it mean to be *walking in the darkness* and *walking in the light?* It seems that John's primary focus was on the consequences of walking in the darkness as opposed to walking in the light rather than explicitly explaining what he meant by these words. However, we can look to the Gospel of John, where he offers us the best definition,

John 3:19-21 Updated American Standard Version (UASV)

[19] And this is the judgment: that the light has come into the world, and men loved the darkness rather than the light, because their works were wicked. [20] For the one who practices wicked things hates the light and does not come to the light, so that his works may not be exposed. [21] But the one who practices the truth comes to the light, in order that his works may be revealed that they are accomplished in God.

One of the themes in The First Epistle of John is the contrast between the one who is practicing sin[77] (walking in the darkness) and the one who

---

[77] I.e., living in sin

is **not** practicing sin (walking in the light). However, even the one not practicing sin may commit a sin because of human imperfection. Nevertheless, he has the ransom sacrifice of Christ to cover over the sin. The apostle Paul tells us in the book of Hebrews, "For if we go on sinning deliberately [walking in darkness] after receiving the accurate knowledge[78] of the truth, there no longer remains a sacrifice for sins [Jesus' ransom sacrifice that covers sin." (Heb. 10:26) Thus, 'walking in the darkness' involves living in sin unrepentantly, while 'walking in the light' involves being declared righteous before God even though a sinner, who sins, but only due to human weaknesses and no serious sins. If he does commit a serious sin, he will be forgiven if he is repentant; thus, Jesus ransom sacrifice will cover that sin. Thus, as we look at the first two chapters, verse-by-verse of John's first epistle, be sure to read the Scriptures as well.

Word of Life

1 John 1:1-4 Updated American Standard Version (UASV)

1 What was from the beginning, what we have heard, what we have seen with our eyes, what we have looked at and touched with our hands, concerning the Word of Life— **2** the life was made manifest, and we have seen it, and testify to it and proclaim to you the eternal life, which was with the Father and was made manifest to us— **3** that which we have seen and heard we proclaim also to you, so that you too may have fellowship[79] with us; and indeed our fellowship is with the Father and with his Son Jesus Christ. **4** And we are writing these things so that our joy may be complete.

John is writing this first letter, sharing the joy that he and other Christians have found in their "fellowship is with the Father and with his Son Jesus Christ." Jesus is "the Word of Life." He was with the Father "in the beginning," wherein he created all things, "in heaven and on earth, visible and invisible." (John 1:1-3; Col. 1:15-16) There were apostates at the time of John's letter, who were rejecting the divinity of Jesus Christ and claiming to be sinless. However, John was one of the main apostles; the one Jesus had loved very much, who spent three and half years traveling with Jesus, saw his execution, resurrection, and ascension. John knew that the Father had "given all authority in heaven and on earth" to the Son. Thousands witnessed the life and ministry of Jesus Christ. Jesus is "the Word of Life" because "the free gift of God is eternal life in Christ Jesus our Lord,"

---

[78] See Romans 3:20 ftn.

[79] Or *a sharing*

85

"who abolished death and brought life." – Romans 6:23; 2 Timothy 1:9-10.

The apostles and other New Testament authors 'proclaimed' that Jesus Christ was sinless, perfect, and divine. John shared these things so that other true Christians 'may also have fellowship with him and other Christians, and indeed their fellowship was with the Father and with his Son Jesus Christ.' (Ps. 133:1-3; John 17:20-21) An apostate is one who not only stands of from the truth, but also turns against those who are truly Christian. Some of these apostates actually believe that they are doing the will of the Father and that they still have a righteous standing before God. They are blinded by their self-righteousness and lack of humility. Other apostates have simply abandoned everything and do not even desire fellowship with the Father and the Son. However, they like the former spend their time attacking their former brothers and sisters.

God Is Light

1 John 1:5-7 Updated American Standard Version (UASV)

[5] This is the message we have heard from him and proclaim to you, that **God is light**, and there is no darkness at all in him. [6] If we say we have fellowship with him and yet we are **walking in the darkness**, we are lying and are not practicing the truth; [7] but if **we are walking in the light**, as he is in the light, we have fellowship with one another, and the blood of Jesus his Son cleanses us from all sin.

John's "message" is what the apostles heard from Jesus. It is "**God is light**,"[80] and there is no darkness at all [nothing unholy, immoral, untrue, or wicked] in him." Therefore, all who are truly Christian will recoil from and turn away from the practice of sin, namely, living in sin.[81] Since certain apostate Christians that accept things like homosexuality being just an

---

[80] "**God is light**. In Scripture, light and darkness are very familiar symbols. Intellectually, light refers to biblical truth, while darkness refers to error or falsehood (cf. Ps. 119:105; Prov. 6:23; John 1:4; 8:12). Morally, light refers to holiness or purity, while darkness refers to sin or wrongdoing (Rom. 13:11–14; 1 Thess. 5:4–7). The heretics claimed to be the truly enlightened, walking in the real light, but John denied that because they do not recognize their sin. About that basic reality, they were unenlightened. no darkness at all. With this phrase, John forcefully affirms that God is absolutely perfect and nothing exists in God's character that impinges upon His truth and holiness (cf. James 1:17)." – MacArthur, John (2005-05-09). *The MacArthur Bible Commentary* (Kindle Locations 65146-65152). Thomas Nelson. Kindle Edition.

[81] See Job 24:14-16; John 3:19-21; Romans 13:11-14; 2 Corinthians 6:14; 1 Thessalonians 5:6-9

alternative lifestyle, which they say God accepts while they are imperfect, these ones do not believe that their works are sinful; therefore, they walk in darkness. They claim to have the true knowledge of Scripture, and in John's day, they claimed to have some secret knowledge. However, being that "God is light," his Word makes known **the truth.** – Matthew 5:14-16; 1 Peter 2:9.

If we believe that we have a part in the fellowship with the Father and the Son but we are **walking in the darkness,** living in sin, "we are lying and are not practicing the truth." However, if are following a life course outlined by an accurate understanding of God's Word, we are **walking in the light,** as God is light. We have "fellowship with [fellow Christians]; and indeed our fellowship is with the Father and with his Son Jesus Christ." This fellowship means that we are one in the biblical truths, our biblical worldview, making disciples, as well as other facets of our pure worship.

Distinct from the apostates, those who are truly Christian, walking in the light, they accept that everything that Bible outlines as sin, in fact, in addition to anything similar to those things, which may not be explicitly mentioned. For example, if Paul exhorted the Ephesian Christians, not to be getting drunk with wine (5:18), it would also apply to getting drunk with whiskey that would not have been available in Paul's day. Again, when John says that the blood of Jesus "cleanses us from all sin," he means every kind of sin. He does not mean the practice of sin. Jesus blood covers Adamic sin, inherited sin, sin from our human weaknesses, but it does not cover living in sin unrepentantly. We are extremely grateful that God make allowances for our imperfection, showing mercy on sinners, who are walking in the light. – Psalm 103:8-14; Micah 7:18-19.

Fellowship with God and the Propitiatory Sacrifice

1 John 1:8-2:2 Updated American Standard Version (UASV)

⁸ If we say we have no sin, we deceive ourselves, and us. ⁹ If we confess our sins, he is faithful and just to forgive us our sins and to cleanse us from all unrighteousness. ¹⁰ If we say we have not sinned, we make him a liar, and his word is not in us.

2 My little children, I am writing these things to you so that you may not commit a sin.[82] But if anyone does sin, we have an advocate with the

---

[82] Gr., *hamartete*, a verb in the aorist subjunctive. According to *A Grammar of New Testament Greek*, by James H. Moulton, Vol. I, 1908, p. 109, "the Aorist has a 'punctiliar' action, that is, it regards action as a *point:* it represents the point of entrance . . . or that of completion . . . or it looks at a whole action simply as having occurred, without distinguishing any steps in its progress."

Father, Jesus Christ the righteous one; ² and he is the propitiation[83] for our sins, and not for ours only but also for the sins of the whole world.

The apostle John informs his readers as to what is needed to be cleansed from sin. This author has had some very long conversations with a person, who claims that Jesus ransom sacrifice has perfected Christians and that they are without sin and can go without sinning. This is absolutely contrary to Scripture and no more so than right here. His claiming to me "he is without sin," is his rejecting the fact that all humans are imperfect and sinful, and "the truth is not in" him. (See 1 Ki 8:46; Eccles. 7:20; Psa. 51:5; Pro. 20:9; Rom. 3:23; 5:12) If he would 'confess his sin, God would be "faith" and 'forgive him of his sins and to cleanse us from all unrighteousness,' and the same holds true for all of us. However, we must have a repentant attitude, which would move us to turn around from and reject wrongdoing. (Pro. 28:13) Of those who are truly Christian, God says, "I will remember their sin no more." (Jer. 31:31-34; Heb. 8:7-12) As to our being forgiven, God is faithful to every promise he makes.

In addition, God is "righteous," at all times adhering to his **standards of justice.** A ransom is a sum of money or a price demanded or paid to secure the freedom of a slave. The basic idea of "ransom" is the act of saving somebody from an oppressed condition or dangerous situation through self-sacrifice, such as a price that *covers* or satisfies justice, while the term "redemption" is the *deliverance* that results from the ransom. In the biblical instance, "redemption" would be the *deliverance* from Adamic sin (the sins of humanity) by the ransom death of Jesus Christ for many.

Hebrew terms (*kāpar, koper, pādâ, gāʾal*), as well as a number of Greek terms (*lytron, antilytron, lytroo, agorazo*), which are translated "ransom and "redeem." They all carry the idea of a price being given or paid to result in a ransom or redemption. In these, there is the sense of an equal or corresponding, that is, a substitution is common in all of these terms. In other words, the ransom sacrifice of Jesus Christ, for example, was given for Adam, which **satisfied justice** and set matters straight between God and man.

Jesus' perfect human life was given as a price to **satisfy justice** and redeem humankind from sin and death. Paul tells us that we "were bought with a price." (1 Cor. 6:20; 7:23) Paul often begins his letters "Paul, a slave of Christ Jesus," as Jesus bought us from Satan the Devil, from condemnation and death, as Peter states, Jesus is the "the Master who bought" us. (Rom. 1:1; 2 Pet. 2.1) Jesus was 'slain, and by his blood, he ransomed [bought] people for God from every tribe and language and

---

[83] Or *an atoning sacrifice; a means of appeasement*

people and nation.' (Rev. 5:9, ESV) Thus, this was a means for God's principal attribute **justice to be satisfied.**

These ones standing off from the truth, say, "we have not sinned," which then 'makes God a liar.' However, 'God cannot lie.' His Word tells us "there is not a righteous man on earth who does good and never sins" (Eccles. 7:20, ESV), "for all have sinned and fall short of the glory of God." (Rom 3:23, ESV) For any, who claim that 'they have not sinned,' this would mean that 'God's his word is not in them.' For those who are truly Christian, 'God has put his laws into their minds, and has written them on their hearts, as he is their God, and they are his people.' – Hebrews 8:10.

John's purpose in penning this letter about sin, forgiveness, and 'cleansing us from all unrighteousness,' is so that his readers may go without practicing sin. While we cannot go without sinning entirely, we can go without living in sin and committing serious sins. (1 Cor. 15:34) Nevertheless, when we do commit "a sin" and are truly repentant, "we have an advocate with the Father, Jesus Christ the righteous one," who pleads with the Father on our behalf. (Heb. 7:26; See John 17:9, 15, 20) Jesus is the propitiation (an atoning sacrifice; a means of appeasement) for our sins. Jesus death satisfied justice, which allowed God to extend mercy and remove Adamic sin for those who are truly Christian. Paul wrote, "For the wages of sin is death, but the free gift of God is eternal life in Christ Jesus our Lord." – Romans 6:23, ESV.

Observing God's Commandments

1 John 2:3-6 Updated American Standard Version (UASV)

³ And by this we know that we have come to know him, if we keep his commandments. ⁴ The one who says, "I have come to know him," and does not keep his commandments, is a liar, and the truth is not in him; ⁵ but whoever keeps his word, truly in this one the love of God has been perfected. By this we know that we are in him: ⁶ the one who says he remains in him ought himself to walk in the same manner as he walked.

If we are to continue our "walking in the light," we must "keep his commandments." Each one of us is responsible for having to 'come to know God,' correctly understanding his qualities and attributes, but also his will and purposes and his commandments. (Matt. 7:21-23) If we claim to know God and at the same time has failed to obey him, he "is a liar." The 'love of God has perfected us,' i.e., made us complete, but only if we obey God's Word. It is by this obedience that 'we know we are in him.' Each of us is obligated to 'walk in the same manner as Jesus walked.' This walking as Jesus did would include our carrying out the commission of proclaiming the Word of God, teaching it, to the point of making disciples. – Matthew 24:14; 28:19-20; Acts 1:8.

The Old and New Commandment

1 John 2:7-8 Updated American Standard Version (UASV)

⁷ Beloved ones, I am writing you, not a new commandment, but an old commandment that you have had from the beginning; the old commandment is the word that you heard. ⁸ Again, I am writing you a new commandment, which is true in him and in you, because the darkness is passing away and the true light is already shining.

John is writing 'an old commandment that his readers in 98 C.E. had from the beginning of when they became Christians. It is "old" because Jesus gave this command fifty-five years earlier, Nisan 14, 33 C.E., when Jesus was foretelling of Peter's denial and how the disciples would abandon in his hour of need. Jesus said, "A new commandment I give to you, that you **love one another**: just as I have loved you, you also are to love one another." It was "new" command in that it went beyond the neighborly love commanded under the Mosaic Law, but now their love required that they be willing to give their life in behalf of their brothers and sisters. (Lev. 19:18; John 15:12-13) It is by this level of self-sacrificing love that Christ had, and we now have that we are in alignment with this new "commandment." Thus, for us, "the darkness is passing away and the true light is already shining."

1 John 2:9-11 Updated American Standard Version (UASV)

⁹ The one who says he is in the light and hates his brother is in the darkness until now. ¹⁰ The one who loves his brother remains in the light and there is no cause for stumbling in him. ¹¹ But the one who hates his brother is in the darkness and walks in the darkness, and does not know where he is going because the darkness has blinded his eyes.

Are we truly in the light? If we say that we are "in the light" and yet, 'we hate our brother,' we are really "in the darkness until now." However, if we love our brother, we remain in the light, and for us "there is no cause for stumbling." The Greek term here, (*skandalon*) originally was "the name of the part of a trap to which the bait is attached, hence, the trap or snare itself." Thus, it is used in "1 John 2:10, "occasion of stumbling," of the absence of this in the case of one who loves his brother and thereby abides in the light. Love, then, is the best safeguard against the woes pronounced by the Lord upon those who cause others to stumble.[84] On this, the Greek-English Lexicon has **"that which causes offense or revulsion and results in opposition, disapproval, or hostility,** *fault, stain* etc.[85] In other words, something that can contribute to one falling into sin. One who claims to be Christian and at the same time hates his brother "does not know where he is going because the darkness has blinded his eyes." (See Matthew 12:35-36) If we heed this warning, we can avoid 'walking in the darkness' by not letting any personal differences get out of control, nor heeding the lies of any who are speaking against the truth or allow anything to hinder our brotherly love.

Reasons for Writing

1 John 2:12-14 Updated American Standard Version (UASV)

[12] I am writing you, little children, because your sins have been forgiven you for the sake of his name. [13] I am writing to you, fathers, because you know him who has been from the beginning. I am writing to you, young men, because you have overcome the evil one. I have written to you, children, because you know the Father. [14] I have written to you, fathers, because you know Him who has been from the beginning. I have written to you, young men, because you are strong, and the word of God remains in you, and you have overcome the evil one.

Here John explains to the "little Children" (i.e., the congregation) why we can have confidence. We can have our sins forgiven 'for the sake of the name of Jesus Christ,' for it is his name alone, by which, we may gain salvation. (Acts 4:12) Those who are truly Christians "know the Father" because they have been begotten by the Holy Spirit (a spiritual rebirth because we were spiritually dead). We see the indwelling of the Holy Spirit as Christians taking the words and ideas of Scripture into our mind and drawing spiritual strength from them. The Spirit moves persons toward salvation, but the Spirit does that, in the same way, any person moves another, by persuasion with words and ideas, i.e., through the Word of God. The "fathers that John addresses, "[knew Jesus] who has been from the beginning," were likely older ones in the congregation, who had more experience and were more mature spiritually.

---

[84] W. E. Vine, Merrill F. Unger, and William White Jr., *Vine's Complete Expository Dictionary of Old and New Testament Words* (Nashville, TN: T. Nelson, 1996), 441.

[85] William Arndt, Frederick W. Danker, and Walter Bauer, *A Greek-English Lexicon of the New Testament and Other Early Christian Literature* (Chicago: University of Chicago Press, 2000), 926.

This would mean, the "young men" were ones who had less experience and were less mature spiritually, yet they "had overcome the evil one." These young ones were not taken advantage by Satan, for they were not ignorant of his schemes. (2 Cor. 2:11) Young ones today should not be ignorant of Satan's schemes either. Satan has set up the world so that it caters to the fallen human flesh. For example, we have unclean entertainment in very large and excessive amounts. Young ones face music that is sensual and some music that is demonic. The internet is filled with pornographic websites. The latest fad is TV shows that portray young vampires, witches, and werewolves as some romantic drama while they carry out murder, black magic, and demonic control. Other TV series have two lesbian mothers over a family of dysfunctional children. The ABC Family channel was one of the biggest offenders of using entertainment to desensitize our young ones into accepting unnatural desires and behaviors as just an alternative lifestyle, which is supposed to be accepted. All of these things can and do erode the Christian mind until it is at odds with the Word of God. To the young, the Bible becomes, a book that is outdated, and the Christian parents are viewed as just not understanding. However, those young ones who are truly Christian will also be victorious over Satan's schemes because they have used the Word of God, family, and the congregation to become spiritually healthy. As John said, "the word of God remains in you, and you have overcome the evil one." The Word of God will help us with any spiritual struggles that we may be facing. Thus, we want to do the same, taking advantage of Bible study tools, rejecting the words of opposers, and actually walking in the light.

A Love We Must Avoid

1 John 2:15-17 Updated American Standard Version (UASV)

15 Do not love the world or the things in the world. If anyone loves the world, the love of the Father is not in him. 16 For all that is in the world, the lust of the flesh and the lust of the eyes and the boastful pride of life, is not from the Father, but is from the world. 17 The world is passing away, and its lusts; but the one who does the will of God remains forever.

It does not matter our age when it comes to the love that we must avoid. John says, "Do not love the world or the things in the world." Satan is the god of this world at present. (2 Cor. 4:3-4) We need 'to keep ourselves unstained from the world,' because "friendship with the world is enmity with God." (Jam. 1:27; 4:4) At one time, "were dead in the trespasses and sins in which you once walked, following the course of this world, following the prince of the power of the air, the spirit that is now at work in the sons of disobedience." (Eph. 2:1-2, ESV) If we had, the mindset or worldview like those alienated from God, or the imitation

Christians, 'the love of the Father would not be in us.' Thus, we certainly need to pray on this matter.

"For all that is in the world" has nothing to do with God or his original purpose for the earth and humans. This definitely includes "the lust of the flesh," which includes unnatural or inappropriate sexual desires. (1 Cor. 6:15-20; Gal. 5:19-21) In addition, we want to avoid "the lust of the eyes." The tree of knowledge in the Garden of Eden had been there for some time and Eve was not tempted by it until Satan put tempting thoughts in her mind. Then, notice how she viewed the tree, "the woman saw that the tree was good for food, and that it was a delight to the eyes, and that the tree was to be desired." (Gen 3:6, ESV) The tree was no different from any of the hundreds of thousands of other fruit trees until Satan made it something that it was not. Then, there was King David watching Bathsheba take baths from his rooftop, who failed to turn away and dismiss the thoughts, which ended up leading to his committing the serious sin of adultery and murder of her husband. (2 Sam. 11:2-17) If we are to continue our walking in the light, we must avoid taking anything into our mind that is morally corrupt. – Proverbs 2:10-22; 4:20-27.

John also spoke of "the boastful pride of life," which is also of this fallen world under satanic influence. One who is proud will boast of his wealth, possessions like house(s), car, clothes, and the like, all of which can go as quickly as it came and has no real lasting value when setting beside eternal life. This one is seeking praise from people, which he may get, but he has no divine praise. – Matthew 6:2, 5, 16, 19-21; James 4:16.

For those who are truly Christian, they keep their eye on the fact that "the world is passing away" (i.e., the wickedness in the world) and those not walking in the light will be destroyed. Yes, the one doing the will of the Father will remain forever. – Matthew 7:21-23; Titus 2:11-14.

Guard Against Anyone In Opposition to the Truth

1 John 2:18-19 Updated American Standard Version (UASV)

[18] Little children, it is the last hour; and just as you heard that antichrist is coming, even now many antichrists have arisen; whereby we know that it is the last hour. [19] They went out from us, but they were not of us; for if they had been of us, they would have continued with us; but they went out, so that they would be revealed that they all are not of us.

We can define antichrist as anyone, any group, any organization, or any government that is *against* or *instead of* Christ, or who mistreat his people. Thus, we are not just looking for one person, one group, one organization, or one power. The Bible does not refer to just one antichrist.

We notice from 1 John 2:18 that it is "the last hour." It is the last hour, because John is almost one hundred years old, and he is the last of the twelve apostles, of the apostolic period, who could protect the Christians from the great apostasy that was coming. We also notice that John says there are "many antichrists." John refers to these collectively as "the antichrist" here in 2 John 1:7. Should Christians be looking for some future time, to identify some specific antichrist? First John was written in the last years of the first century, about 98 C.E., and yet John says that there were antichrists already in the world during his day. It is the signs of antichrists in John's day, which let him, know it was the last hour. What characteristics do the antichrists have?

Psalm 2:2 American Standard Version (ASV)

2 The kings of the earth take their stand

The kings of the earth take their stand,
   and the rulers take counsel together,
   against Jehovah and against his anointed one [Messiah, or Christ,
saying,

Matthew 24:24 Updated American Standard Version (UASV)

24 For **false Christs** and false prophets will arise and will show great signs and wonders, so as to mislead, if possible, even the chosen ones.

1 John 2:22 Updated American Standard Version (UASV)

22 Who is the liar but the one who denies that Jesus is the Christ? This is **the antichrist**, even the one who denies the Father and the Son.

1 John 4:3 Updated American Standard Version (UASV)

3 and every spirit that does not confess Jesus is not from God; this is the spirit of the antichrist, of which you have heard that it is coming, and now it is **in the world already**.

2 John 1:7 Updated American Standard Version (UASV)

7 For **many** deceivers have gone out into the world, even those who do not confess the coming of Jesus Christ in the flesh. This is the deceiver and **the antichrist**.

Thus, it would be any person, group, organization, or power, who

- The antichrist denies that Jesus is the Christ,

- The antichrist denies the Father and the Son,

- Some of the antichrist have abandoned the Christian faith, and thereafter work in opposition to Christ,

- The antichrist is anti-Christian

In our main text 1 John 2:18-19, John is reminding his readers that the apostles had warned them that the antichrist is coming. The appearance of many antichrists at the end of the first-century and just before the death of the last apostle was evidence it was the last hour, the close of the apostolic period. The ones who are against Christ are a composite antichrist, just as we showed the man of lawlessness is a composite. The composite antichrist is made up of different ones who pretend to be worshipers of God, but as John said, "They went out from us, but they were not of us," as they abandoned the truth. We are not distraught over the loss of these ones, as their removing themselves or being removed from those that are truly Christian, serves as a protection of the congregation.

1 John 2:20-21 Updated American Standard Version (UASV)

20 But you have been anointed by the Holy One, and you all have knowledge. 21 I have not written to you because you do not know the truth, but because you do know it, and because no lie is of the truth.

Those who are truly Christian 'have been anointed by the Holy One, and they all have knowledge about those who would be against Christ and his people. They have bought out the time to understand the Word of God correctly, knowing the truth as it relates to Jesus Christ. The apostates, on the other hand, have incorrect views of Christ. We know that "no lie is of the truth," all who love the Father and obey his Word reject views that are biblically untrue and those presenting them.

1 John 2:22-25 Updated American Standard Version (UASV)

22 Who is the liar but the one who denies that Jesus is the Christ? This is the antichrist, even the one who denies the Father and the Son. 23 Everyone who denies the Son does not have the Father; the one who confesses the Son has the Father also. 24 As for you, let that remain in you which you heard from the beginning. If what you heard from the beginning remains in you, you also will remain in the Son and in the Father. 25 And this is the promise which he himself promised us: eternal life.

In the end, "who is the liar but the one who denies that Jesus is the Christ," the Father's Anointed One?

As we have learned, anyone denying the Father and the Son is the antichrist. When these ones deny the truth of God's Word, we should not even associate with them, nor use them as a source on other biblical topics that they may have correct. If a Bible scholar quotes another Bible scholar as a source, when this scholar has repeatedly published material that questions full or absolute inerrancy of Scripture, it only serves to give this pseudo-scholar validity and credibility. Yes, some scholars such as agnostic

Dr. Bart D. Ehrman are prominent New Testament professors in leading universities, working in a major field like New Testament textual criticism, but they should be shunned as an enemy of Christ. When you coauthor books with such ones, it gives unsuspecting Christians the beliefs that it is safe to read their books. No to mention, do we really want to coauthor a book with the antichrist?

Only true Christians "honor the Son, just as they honor the Father. Whoever does not honor the Son does not honor the Father who sent him." (John 5:23)[86] So, if we correctly 'acknowledge Jesus before men, he also will acknowledge us before my Father who is in heaven, but the apostates who deny Jesus before men, he also will deny them before his Father who is in heaven.' (Matt. 10:32-33) The first century Christians clung to what they had heard about the Son of the Father "from the beginning" of their Christian lives. If we truly 'know the only, true God, and Jesus Christ whom the Father sent, we can look forward to eternal life.' – John 17:3

Taught by God

1 John 2:26-29 Updated American Standard Version (UASV)

[26] These things I have written to you concerning the ones who are trying to deceive you. [27] As for you, the anointing which you received from him remains in you, and you have no need for anyone to teach you; but as his anointing teaches you about all things, and is true and is not a lie, and just as it has taught you, you remain in him.

[28] And now, little children, remain in him, so that when He appears we may have confidence[87] and not be ashamed before him at his coming. [29] If you know that he is righteous, you also know that everyone who practices righteousness has been born from him.

If we are going to continue our walking in the light and not be fooled by apostates, we need to have an accurate knowledge of God's Word. Sadly, the spark of interest that was at the beginning of our walking with God grew stagnant for many, meaning that their spiritual growth died out. They had deceived themselves that they were healed from the old person, and so they grew apathetic in their prayer, personal Bible study and their

---

[86] Kenneth O. Gangel writes, "Anyone who does not recognize that authority in the Son has denied the authority of the Father—the very authority to give life. The phrase who sent him at the end of verse 23 is used by the Lord only of the Father" (4:34; 5:24, 30; 6:38–39; 7:16, 28, 33; 8:26, 29; 9:4; 12:44–45; 13:20; 15:21; 16:5). (K. O. Gangel 2000, p. 102)

[87] Gr., *parresia*; Lit., "freedom of speech" "outspokenness"

application of what they were learning, as well as their Christian meeting attendance. In time, they suffered a relapse into the old person they were. In some case, they became more spiritually sick than they had been. They opened themselves up to the wiles of Satan and his demons, which are very eager to take advantage of their missteps. This should concern every one of us as we walk with God throughout this evil age we live in, as it is a battle between the light and the darkness.

The Holy Bible that we have is the inspired, inerrant Word of God, and is compared to "eye salve to anoint your eyes so that you may see." (Rev 3:18) This likely reminds of Jesus applied spit that he had mixed with dirt when he miraculously healed a blind man. (John 9:1–12). At that time, he told his opponents, "If you were blind, you would have no sin; but since you say, 'We see,' your sin remains." (John 9:41) Are we going to be like the Laodicean church, believing that we have spiritual insight if we are spiritually weak or have grown spiritually weak? Alternatively, we could recognize our spiritual apathy, 'so that we may be filled with the knowledge of his will in all spiritual wisdom and understanding.' (Col. 1:9) Jesus prayed to the Father, "Sanctify them in the truth; your word is truth." (John 17:17) Jesus had told the Samaritan woman at the well, "true worshipers will worship the Father in spirit and truth, for the Father is seeking such people to worship him." – John 4:23.

"So God created man in his own image, in the image of God he created him; male and female he created them." (Gen. 1:27) While we are imperfect, we still reflect the qualities of God, such as wisdom, love and justice. Unlike the animals, we have the mental powers and ability to reason, which enables us to see the significance of our Creator's qualities that we too possess in a small measure and are able to use for our own good. The Scriptures describe the mental powers and ability to reason by the use of the words *mind* and *conscience*.

Having the Right Mind

The *mind* is the center of consciousness that generates thoughts, feelings, ideas, and perceptions, and stores knowledge and memories. It gives us the capacity to think, understand, and reason. It also gives us concentration, or the ability to concentrate. The Bible uses the term mind in several different ways. One such way the Bible uses the term *mind* is that of taking in knowledge, with the capacity to think, understand, and reason, helping us to arrive at certain conclusions. For example, one might say when studying this book, 'I am trying to keep my mind on You Must Love the Lord chapter.' What would we mean by that statement? We would mean that we are trying to keep our minds alert, concentrating, and observant to take in all the information contained therein. This **thought** process is the activity of thinking, i.e., ideas, plans, conceptions, or beliefs produced by the **mental activity**. In speaking of the Bereans, Paul said, "Now these Jews were more noble than those in Thessalonica; they received the word with all eagerness [Gr., *prothumias*, **readiness of mind**],[88] examining the Scriptures daily to see if these things were so." Simon J. Kistemaker in *Exposition of the Acts of the Apostles* writes,

> The reason for the openness of the Bereans lies in their receptivity to and love for God's Word. For them, the Scriptures are much more than a written scroll or book that conveys a divine message. They use the Old Testament as the touchstone of truth, so that when Paul proclaims the gospel they immediately go to God's written Word for verification. They do so, Luke adds, with great eagerness. Note well, the adjective *great* indicates that they treasure the Word of God. Luke ascribes the same diligence to the Bereans as Peter does to the Old Testament prophets, who intently and diligently searched the Word and inquired into its meaning (1 Peter 1:10). The Bereans open the Scriptures and with ready minds learn that Jesus has fulfilled the messianic prophecies.[89]

Another such way that the Bible uses the term *mind* is the ability store the knowledge we have taken in and reasoned upon in our memories. For example, when we such things as, "I will keep that in mind," which means that we will store them in our memory, for future recall. The apostle Paul wrote to Titus saying, "Remind them to be submissive to rulers and authorities, to be obedient, to be ready for every good work." This ability is yet another way that we are made in the image of God, as Jeremiah tells his readers,

Jeremiah 44:21 Updated American Standard Version (UASV)

[21] "As for the smoking sacrifices that you burned in the cities of Judah and in the streets of Jerusalem, you and your forefathers, your kings and your princes, and the people of the land, did not Jehovah **remember** them and did not *all this* **come into his mind**?

Within our *mind* is the capacity to think, understand, and reason about the knowledge (i.e., information in mind) which we have acquired, enabling us to make decisions. It depends on the information taken in, as to whether our decision will be wise or unwise. Paul exhorted the

---

[88] W. E. Vine, Merrill F. Unger, and William White Jr., *Vine's Complete Expository Dictionary of Old and New Testament Words* (Nashville, TN: T. Nelson, 1996), 508.

[89] http://biblia.com/books/bkrc-ac/Page.p_621

Corinthians that they "all agree and that there be no divisions among you, but that you be made complete in the same mind and in the same judgment." (1 Cor. 1:10)[90] In other words, they were to come to the same biblical truths. Paul told the Romans, "For those who live according to the flesh set their minds on the things of the flesh, but those who live according to the Spirit set their minds on the things of the Spirit." (Rom 8:5) Those in the world, who are alienated from God, but who still have a measure of *conscience*, which can determine right from wrong, entertain wrong thinking on the fallen flesh, awakening wrong desires, which affects their course of action. If they entertain wrong thinking and follow wrong desires for a time, they will begin to build a mindset and a pattern of behavior. This over time, left unchecked, will eventually lead to a personality that is very much at odds with God. When an unbeliever finds God, and becomes a Christian, he will need a completely new mindset and a pattern of behavior. Concerning this, Paul said,

Romans 12:2 New American Standard Bible (NASB)	Colossians 3:9-10 Lexham English Bible (LEB)
2 And do not be conformed to this world, but be transformed by the renewing of your mind, so that you may prove what the will of God is, that which is good and acceptable and perfect.	9 Do not lie to one another, *because you* have taken off the old man together with his deeds, 10 and have put on the new *man* that is being renewed in knowledge according to the image of the one who created him,

Humans have the capacity of having various attitudes of mind. When we think of a high-minded person, this is a prideful person. Then, again, if we are thinking of a humble-minded person, this is a person, who has a modest and unassuming in attitude about himself. The latter here is the mental attitude that Jesus had. In fact, Paul counseled the Philippians to "Have this mind among yourselves, which is yours in Christ Jesus." (Phil. 2:5) Peter also says, "Since therefore Christ suffered in the flesh, arm yourselves with the same way of thinking." (1 Pet 4:1) The word *spirit* can refer to one's will or sense of self, or somebody's personality or temperament. This is largely influenced by the mind.

---

[90] "1:10 **speak the same thing**. Paul is emphasizing the unity of doctrine in the local assembly of believers, not the spiritual unity of His universal church. Doctrinal unity, clearly and completely based on Scripture, must be the foundation of all church life (cf. John 17:11, 21–23; Acts 2:46, 47). Both weak commitment to doctrine and commitment to disunity of doctrine will severely weaken a church and destroy the true unity. In its place, there can be only shallow sentimentalism or superficial harmony." – MacArthur, John (2005-05-09). *The MacArthur Bible Commentary* (Kindle Locations 53053-53056). Thomas Nelson. Kindle Edition.

Proverbs 25:28 American Standard Version (ASV)

²⁸ He whose spirit [personality or temperament] is without restraint is like a city that is broken down and without walls.⁹¹

However, we are blessed with another loving gift, another mental power from our heavenly Father at the creation of Adam and Eve. Looking again at Genesis 1:27 it says, "God created man in his own image, in the image of God he created him; male and female he created them," which means that man is born with a moral nature, which creates within him a conscience that reflects God's moral values. (Rom 2:14-15) It acts as a moral law within. Even in imperfection, we are born with a measure of that conscience, which can be developed toward good or bad. A Christian conscience is developed by the Word of God. Paul told Titus,

Titus 1:15 Updated English Standard Version (UASV)

¹⁵ To the pure [persons with a conscience guided by the Bible], all things are pure; but to those who are defiled and unbelieving, nothing is pure, but both their minds [mental power] and their consciences are defiled.

We have to appreciate and realize that even after we take on the new person that Paul spoke of, as well as the mind of Christ, we will still be affected by our inborn leanings of a sinful nature. Really, there is a battle because waging between the two.

Romans 7:21-25 Updated English Standard Version (UASV)

²¹ I find then the law in me that when I want to do right, that evil is present in me. ²² For I delight in the law of God according to the inner man, ²³ but I see a different law in my members, warring against the law of my mind and taking me captive in the law of sin which is in my members. ²⁴ Wretched man that I am! Who will deliver me from this body of death? ²⁵ Thanks be to God through Jesus Christ our Lord! So then, I myself serve the law of God with my mind, but with my flesh, I serve the law of sin.

The good news is that if a person is walking with Christ and according to Scripture, he will no longer be a slave to sin. The sinful leaning will be there, but as long as it is not fed, it will not dominate his life. He will no longer have a life that feeds the beast, such as inappropriate music, television, internet viewing, associations, thinking, and so on. This will give him a clean conscience before God, knowing that he now has a righteous

---

⁹¹ "**25:28 city broken down.** Such are exposed and vulnerable to the incursion of evil thoughts and successful temptations." – MacArthur, John (2005-05-09). *The MacArthur Bible Commentary* (Kindle Locations 25729-25730). Thomas Nelson. Kindle Edition.

standing, and all his past has been forgiven, cast behind the back of God. There may come times in his life when his sinful nature will attempt to reassert itself, and he will have to take steps of dismissing any wrongful thinking, replacing it with rational Scriptural thinking, as well as intensive prayer, even speaking with a spiritually mature one within the congregation.

Having the Right Heart

The term *heart* as it is commonly used in the Bible is very much related to this discussion. God is not interested in our outward appearances, but rather the inner man and woman. (1 Sam. 16:7) God's Word tells its reader, "The refining pot is for silver and the furnace is for gold, and Jehovah **tests hearts**." (Pro. 17:3) If we want to be clean in the eyes of the one who examines our heart; then, we must guard against what we take into our heart. Proverbs also says, "If you say, 'Behold, we did not know this,' does not he who **weighs the heart** perceive it? Does not he who keeps watch over your soul know it, and will he not repay man according to his work?" (Pro. 24:12) God can examine our hearts, and he can read our minds, as he knows our very thoughts, and he will know if we are indifferent toward him. The Scriptures also counsels, "Keep your heart [inner person] with all diligence, for out of it flow the springs of life." (Pro. 4:23) The feelings of love, hate, and everything in between, flow from the human heart, which is the inner person, meaning it is about "life" and death. In other words, how we develop our heart, will be indicative of whether we receive eternal life or not.

The Bible also uses the word "heart" in such a context that it is referring to our *mental power.* Moses pressed the Israelites, "Lay it to your heart [your mind] that Jehovah is God." In addition, later he told them, "Jehovah has not given you a heart [mind] to know." (Deut. 4:39; 29:4) Whether we are talking about the Hebrew Old Testament or the Greek New Testament, the *heart* is associated with our intellect and thinking. Speaking to some of the scribes, "Jesus, knowing their thoughts, said, 'Why do you think evil in your hearts?'" (Matt 9:4) We are told by Mark 2:6, "some of the scribes were sitting there and reasoning in their hearts." Mark 6:52 says, "For they did not understand about the loaves, but their hearts were hardened."

An overview of Scripture would reveal that God in the Old Testament was searching for right-hearted ones (Enoch, Noah, Abraham, Moses, Joshua, Daniel, Jeremiah, etc.), and in the New Testament he has his disciples searching for right-hearted ones, ones with a receptive heart (Cornelius, Lydia, Onesimus, etc.). He is very much interested in our intentions of the heart, love, reasons, steadfast-faith and affection. When we feed our minds on the Word of God, in serious personal Bible study, of the deeper things of God, as we are doing now, we are planting seeds in the soil of our heart (Matt 13:23). This strengthens us against our own imperfect flesh, the world that caters to that flesh, and against Satan and his horde of demons. When the Spirit inspired, inerrant Word of God grows in our heart, it develops the fruitage of the Spirit (Gal. 5:22-23). What may be grown in our hearts in personal Bible study, in preparation for our meetings, and the attendance of meetings will grow twentyfold if we are actively sharing Bible truths with others. Seeds of truth are reinforced and planted even deeper, so doubt cannot get at them (Jude 1:3, 22). The Psalmist tells us, "Be strong, and let your heart take courage, all you who hope in Jehovah." (Psa. 31:24, ASV) Spiritual strength and maturity are not instantaneous, like being born again; rather they are based on our buying out the time to develop them. – Proverbs 2:1-6.

Those who allow themselves to remain spiritual babes (Heb. 5:12-6:1) are (1) making themselves vulnerable to Satanic attacks, (2) deviation from the faith by way of human weaknesses, and (3) doubt, i.e., spiritual sickness. While it is true that "the god of this world has blinded the minds of the unbelievers," he also has **the ability to close the mind of** believers (1 Pet. 5:8), if he is given entry through the wall that protects us, a wall of protection, which exists only through the Father, the Son and the Holy Spirit. (Job 1:10-12) We 'were once alienated and hostile in mind, doing evil deeds,' have now been reconciled to God (Col. 1:21), "to present you holy and blameless and above reproach before him." (Col. 1:22) Remember Adam and Eve, who were perfect in mind and body, and had the natural desire toward good. Yes, we do well to heed the words of Paul to the Corinthians and the Ephesians,

---

2 Corinthians 11:3 Updated American Standard Version (UASV)

[3] But I am afraid that, as the serpent deceived Eve by his craftiness, your minds will be led astray from a sincerity and pure devotion to Christ.

Ephesians 6:14 Updated American Standard Version (UASV)	**Ephesians 6:17** Updated American Standard Version (UASV)
[14] Stand firm, therefore, with your loins girded[92] about with truth,	[17] And take the helmet of salvation, and the sword of the Spirit, which is the word of God.

---

[92] (an idiom, literally 'to gird up the loins') to cause oneself to be in a state of readiness–'to get ready, to prepare oneself.'–GELNTBSD

and having put on the breastplate of righteousness,	

Psalm 139:23-24 Updated American Standard Version (UASV)

²³ Search me, O God, and know my heart;
   Examine me, and know my anxious⁹³ thoughts;
²⁴ And see whether there is in me any painful way,⁹⁴
   And lead me in the everlasting way

Review Questions

- Does Jesus' blood enable us to go without sinning?

- Who is the ultimate source of life?

- What does it mean to pass over from death to life? Does this mean that it will be fast and easy to give up our old ways?

- What is needed in order to be cleansed from sin?

- How has justice been satisfied?

- Why is a person's claim to be a Christian false if he hates his brother?

- Why can we have confidence?

- What love must we avoid and why?

- What is the correct understanding of the antichrist?

- How should we view Bible scholars and teachers that work with apostates?

- How are we taught by God?

- What is meant by having the right mind?

- What does it mean to have the right heart?

- What can happen if we are not working toward doing the things⁹⁵ that will help us maintain our spirituality?

---

⁹³ Or *disquieting*

⁹⁴ Or *hurtful way*

⁹⁵ Paul said that we "work out our salvation" (Phil. 2:12), James said, "a person is justified by works and not by faith alone" (Jam 2:24), and he said, "faith apart from works is dead." (Jam 2:26) This of course, does not mean that we earn

- What is one way that the Bible uses the term mind?

- What is another way that the Bible uses the term mind?

- What determines whether we will make a good or bad decision?

- How do those in the world end up with a personality that is very much at odds with God?

- Of the various attitudes of mind, which one should we imitate?

- As imperfect humans, we lean toward sin. What will enable us to avoid sinning?

- What role does the heart play in this discussion?

- How are we to understand Proverbs 4:23?

- Who reads our hearts? How are our figurative hearts strengthened?

- Whom is Satan seeking?

- What strengthens our minds and hearts?

---

our salvation through works, but that our works are an evident demonstration of our faith. We cannot have faith without having works.

CHAPTER 9 Jesus Will Come to Call the Righteous

Luke 5:32 Updated American Standard Version (UASV)

³² "I have not come to call the righteous but sinners to repentance."

Repentance is a fundamental teaching within God's Word, along with such basics as faith, baptism, and atonement. The importance of repentance is seen in the fact that one cannot receive the gift of salvation without it. – Hebrews 6:1-2.

According to the *Encarta Dictionary*, repents means "to recognize the wrong in something you have done and be sorry about it," or "to feel regret about a sin or past actions and change your ways or habits." The *Holman Illustrated Dictionary* has,

> Change of mind; also can refer to regret or remorse accompanying a realization that wrong has been done or to any shift or reversal of thought. In its biblical sense repentance refers to a deeply seated and thorough turning from self to God. It occurs when a radical turning to God takes place, an experience in which God is recognized as the most important fact of one's existence.

> **Old Testament** The concept of a wholehearted turning to God is widespread in the preaching of the OT prophets. Terms such as "return," turn," or "seek" are used to express the idea of repentance.

> In Amos 4–5 the Lord sends judgment in order for the nation to return to Him. Corporate repentance of the nation is a theme in Hosea (Hos. 6:1; 14:2) and the result of Jonah's preaching to Nineveh (Jon. 3:10). Classic calls to repentance are found in Ezek. 18 and 33 as well as Isa. 55. The shift toward an emphasis on individual repentance can be seen in Ezek. 18.

> **New Testament** Repentance was the keynote of the preaching of John the Baptist, referring to a complete turn from self to God. A note of urgency is attached to the message, "The kingdom of heaven has come near!" (Matt. 3:2 HCSB). Those who were prepared to make such a radical reorientation of their lives demonstrated that by being baptized (Mark 1:4). This complete redirection of their lives was to be demonstrated by profound changes in lifestyle and relationships (Luke 3:8–14).

> The emphasis upon a total life change continues in the ministry of Jesus. The message of repentance was at the heart of

His preaching (Mark 1:15). When describing the focus of His mission, Jesus said, "I have not come to call the righteous, but sinners to repentance" (Luke 5:32 HCSB).

The call to repentance is a call to absolute surrender to the purposes of God and to live in this awareness. This radical turning to God is required of all people: "Unless you repent, you will all perish" (Luke 13:3). Those who had witnessed the ministry of Jesus, the reality of God, and His claims on their lives faced serious jeopardy if they failed to repent. Jesus warned of serious consequences for those where His ministry had been rejected: "He proceeded to denounce the towns where most of His miracles were done, because they did not repent" (Matt. 11:20 HCSB). On the other hand, for the one sinner who repents, there is great "joy in heaven" (Luke 15:7). In His final words to the disciples, Jesus demanded that the same message of repentance He had preached would be preached to all nations (Luke 24:47).

What Truths and Principles

If we are going to appreciate fully what all is involved in repentance, as far as God is concerned, we have to get at the truth and principles of biblical repentance. **The first task** of those who are truly Christian is to accept, based on an accurate knowledge and understanding that God does exist, and he is the Creator and owner of his people. Moreover, he is the Sovereign of the universe, the Most High, the Judge, the Lawgiver, and so justice must always be satisfied. This should not be frightening, as if we are before an earthly judge, governor, or world leader, with their fickle emotions. Some of the other major qualities of our Creator are love, kindness, mercy, and patience, to mention just a few. Nevertheless, we are accountable to our Creator as should be expected. Being that we were given free will, as well as an internal conscience that enables us to distinguish between right and wrong, we are accountable for our actions, as well as our thoughts and feelings that lead to our actions. In other words, God is so far more superior than his angelic creation; it is not even really conceivable to the human creation, which is far more inferior than the angels just how infinite our Creator's qualities are. Therefore, if some human government has the capacity to determine laws that hold us morally accountable, how much more so would this be true of God? This basic truth seems to escape the agnostic and atheist.

The second task of those who are truly Christian is to come to terms with the fact that humanity has inherited sin from Adam, and just what his sinful condition entrails. Adam and Eve in the Garden of Eden had free will but chose to abuse it and to rebel against their Creator. God had created them perfect; they lacked nothing. They need not fear any illnesses, hunger, death, any form of difficulty that plagues man today. The only requirement that they had was to live out their freedom under the sovereignty of God, i.e., the righteous rule of God, and the laws that the Creator would introduce, including the laws of nature.

One such natural law was that they would grow hungry if they did not eat, thus the need to obey the law to eat. The same would hold true for water as well, and the need to drink. Then, there was a need for sleep. Outside of these natural laws, God gave them work to accomplish within Eden, yet we will note in the texts below, there were not innumerable details, rules, and regulations. They had the freedom to fulfill the work that was assigned, as long as it was fulfilled.

However, one must recognize that the freedom given to a child to make decisions on their own means they are given responsibilities, and they are trusted to carry out those responsibilities. Moreover, it does not mean that the act of decision making alone, for the sake of making them, are going to end with good results. A child must learn and grow from being taught by their father and mother, and as they demonstrate that, they are ready for more freedom and responsibility; then, they will receive it. God did not create Adam and Eve so that there was no need for growth, no need to learn. He gave both man and woman intelligence so that they could grow in knowledge and understanding, wisely making application to what they were learning. Of both Adam and Eve God said, "Let us make man in our image, after our likeness." This means that the inner person within the first human pair would have possessed the same qualities in their decision-making skills as their Creator. If their love and respect for God and all he had done grew, it would have only been natural that they would have wanted to please him.

There was one law that the first couples were given, which would allow them to evidence their love and appreciation, as well as grow from their experience of obeying this law. "And Jehovah God commanded the man, saying, 'From every tree of the garden you may freely eat, but of the tree of the knowledge of good and evil you shall not eat, for in the day that you eat of it, you shall surely die.'" (Gen. 2:16-17) They had an entire Garden of trees to eat from, as "God caused to grow every tree that was pleasing to the sight and good for food." (Gen. 2:9) What did this mean? It meant that they lacked nothing regardless of this one restricted tree. It also meant that to obey or not obey was within their free will, and they were no lacking of anything that would have contributed to their disobeying. Nevertheless, Adam, who was to be the father of humankind,

meaning that he had to learn that while he was given the earth as his domain, it still belonged to God as the rightful Ruler. – Psalm 24:1, 10.

Born Into Slavery: Did you know that we are all born slaves? The facts are quite staggering to the first-time hearer; all humans were/are slaves and born of slaves. Each of us must face the facts, by looking honestly at the truthful evidence before us, which will help us to appreciate many things about man that have only been a mystery before first century Christianity. More importantly, it will help each of us to understand that while we may be born into slavery, a provision has paid that will release us from this bondage.

When the first man Adam willfully chose to disobey God's law, he gave up possession of perfect control of himself, gave into his selfish desire to continue with his wife, and placed her above his Creator, Jehovah God. His giving into this sinful desire made it and the result thereof, sin, his taskmaster, leading him as a slave. (Rom 6:16; James 1:14-15) In essence, he chose to place himself under sin. Sadly, all of humankind was yet to be born; therefore, Adam sold his future descendants under sin. It is for this reason that the Apostle Paul could write: "For we know that the law is spiritual, but I am of the flesh, sold under sin." (Rom 7:14) It is for this alone that humans were without a means of returning to perfection, unable to keep God's righteous Law given through Moses. The Apostle Paul put it this way: "The very commandment that promised life proved to be death to me." (Rom 7:10) What the Mosaic Law had accomplished was to highlight their inability to keep this law perfectly, labeling them as slaves to sin (missing the mark of perfection), and deserving death. Exactly, what is sin though? Sin is anything not in harmony with God's personality, standards, ways, will, and purpose.[96]

The lost opportunity for eternal life on a paradise earth, humankind walking with God in peace, took place when the first man, Adam, in an act of disobedience and rebellion, sinned against God. However, all was not lost, because there was one perfect man, who could recover this walking with God in peace, and the hope of eternal life, Christ Jesus, the second Adam, regaining through obedience, what Adam had lost through disobedience.

- Death by One Man (Rom. 5:12)

- From Adam to Moses (Rom. 5:13-14)

- Adam's Sin Contrasted with the Gift of Christ (Rom. 5:15)

---

[96] (See Job 2:10; Psa. 39:1; Lev. 20:20; 2 Cor. 12:21; Pro 21:4; Rom. 3:9-18; 2 Pe 2:12-15; Heb. 3:12, 13, 18, 19)

- Adam's Condemnation Contrasted with the Righteousness of Christ (Rom. 5:16)

- The Reign of Death Contrasted With the Reign of Life (Rom. 5:17)

As with the ripple effect of a rock thrown into a pond, it took one man to create the ripple effect of all of humankind being placed into slavery, sold, sinful, ending with death. Fortunately, two of God's cardinal attributes is wisdom and power, using these; he was able to make the needed arrangements of offering another Adam, Jesus Christ, as a means of repurchasing humankind. It is here in verses 12–18 that we see his third chief attribute of justice being used in bringing into balance one man against another man in this repurchasing process, maintaining just all along the way.

This one act of disobedience to his God was a transgression, a sinning by "overstepping," 'sidestepping,' "bypassing," or 'passing beyond' (Heb., 'avar) God's covenant or specific orders.[97] (See Num. 14:41; Deut. 17:2, 3; Josh 7:11, 15; 1 Sam 15:24; Isa 24:5; Jer. 34:18) Therefore, Adam was guilty of sin. It is by means of inheritance that the descendants of Adam came into sin. From the time of the birth of Adam's firstborn son up unto the giving of the Mosaic Law, there was no law code; therefore, man was unable to transgress in the way of Adam.

From Genesis up unto the baptism of Christ Jesus, there was a mystery of who the prophesied seed would be. (Gen 3:15) It was not until the apostle Paul that Jesus was truly disclosed as this 1,500-year-old mystery. We find that Jesus is the second Adam, who bore some resemblance to the first, in that both were perfect humans. The first Adam committed a trespass when he very well could have chosen not to, which lead to sickness, old age, and death. On the other hand, the second Adam [Jesus] was perfectly obedient under much more severe trials, which would lead to any who trust in him receiving an unearned righteous standing for an imperfect person, and the hope of eternal life, two entirely different courses.

As was already stated, the first Adam committed his one "trespass" in the Garden of Eden, causing the death sentence of all his descendants up unto the first century C.E. It is here that man receives the unearned, the undeserved gift of "that one man Jesus Christ." By means of this "one man," God's righteous requirement of justice is met, giving many an opportunity once again to walk with Him in an approved condition. This undeserved gift was so effective that even Enoch and Noah could be spoken

---

[97] Harris, R. Laird; Harris, Robert Laird; Archer, Gleason Leonard; Waltke, Bruce K.: *Theological Wordbook of the Old Testament.* electronic ed. Chicago: Moody Press, 1999, c1980, S. 640

of as though they were walking with God based on their faith in this coming one. Here is the similarity, for both have an impact on the many.

In other words, the judgment of condemnation by God came from Adam's one trespass. This one trespass brought Adam and all who were yet to be born under the condemnation of death. In Galatians 3:19, the Apostle Paul informs us that the law "was added because of transgressions until the offspring should come to whom the promise had been made." In other words, the Mosaic Law was added to highlight the sinful nature of man and the need for a greater sacrifice. When God gave the Law to Moses, there were "many trespasses" on the part of the Israelites, establishing that humankind is sinful and in need of something more than animal sacrifices. The "free gift" allowed God's justice to be met, offering all who has an active faith [i.e., complete trust] in that gift, to be declared righteous, although imperfect.

The "trespass of the one man" is a sin of encroaching on his Creator's righteous standards of right and wrong, to decide for him what is right and wrong, rejecting the sovereignty of the one who created him. The penalty of death was made clear to this "one man." The trespass of Adam in the Garden of Eden brought the reign of death to not only himself, but also all who would come out of his loins. On the opposite end of the scale is the unearned, undeserved gift of God, the free gift of righteousness, pulling any who accepted this free gift out of the quagmire of sin and death! This "free gift of righteousness" enables all who accept it to "reign in life." This hope that is set before all is a result of the sacrifice of the "one man Jesus Christ."

Initially, Adam and Eve's mental disposition or inclination was not toward evil or bad, sin. Hence, while imperfect humans are inclined, lean toward wrongdoing, it was just the opposite for our first human parents; their natural inclination was toward doing good. This is just the opposite of their descendants, for we have inherited the disease of sin, missing the mark, or standard of perfection. (Gen. 6:5, AT) "When the Lord saw that the wickedness of man on the earth was great and that the whole bent of his thinking was never anything but evil ..." (Gen. 8:21, AT) " ... the bent of man's mind may be evil from his very youth ..." (Jer. 17:9) "The heart is deceitful above all things, and it is exceedingly corrupt: who can know it?"

The Man We Are Inside

(John 13:35) [35] By this all people will know that you are my disciples, if you have love for one another." "Disciple," "pupil," "student" and "learner: (One who loves discipline) *mathetes*

(1 John 1:8) [8] If we say we have no sin, we deceive ourselves, and the truth is not in us. "Sin," "miss" hamartia (Missing the mark of perfection)

(Rom 7:22) ²² For I delight in the law of God, in my inner being. "The inside man," "the man I am within," "inward being," "inward man" *ton eso anthropos*

(Eph. 4:23) ²³ and to be renewed in the spirit of your minds. Lit. "The spirit of the mind" "made new in the force actuating your mind," "renewed in the spirit of your mind,"

(Eph. 2:15) ¹⁵ by abolishing the law of commandments expressed in ordinances, that he might create in himself one new man in place of the two, so making peace. Lit. "New man," "new self," "new personality"

(1 Co 2:14) ¹⁴ The natural person does not accept the things of the Spirit of God, for they are folly to him, and he is not able to understand them because they are spiritually discerned. (The natural person seeks only the desire of his fallen flesh, ignoring his spiritual needs.)

(Rom 8:6-7) ⁶ For to set the mind on the flesh is death, but to set the mind on the Spirit is life and peace. ⁷ For the mind that is set on the flesh is hostile to God, for it does not submit to God's law; indeed, it cannot. Lit, "minding," 'way of thinking, mindset, aim, aspiration, striving.' *phronema*

When we couple our leaning toward wrongdoing with the fact that Satan the devil, who is "the god of this world," (2 Co 4:4) has worked to entice these leanings, the desires of the fallen flesh; we are even further removed from our relationship with our loving heavenly Father. During these 'last days, grievous times' has fallen on us as Satan is working all the more to prevent God's once perfect creation to achieve a righteous standing with God and entertaining the hope of eternal life. – 2 Timothy 3:1-5.

Our conscience thinking (aware) and subconscious thinking (present in our mind without you being aware of it) originates in the mind. For good, or for bad, our mind follows certain rules of action, which if entertained one will move even further in that direction until they are eventually consumed for good or for bad. In our imperfect state, our bent thinking will lean toward wrong, especially with Satan using his world of fallen humans, with so many forms of entertainment that merely feeds the flesh. – James 1:14-15.

Scriptural repentance demanded that there was some provision by which or some basis upon which God can make certain that justice is satisfied and yet take awareness of repentance, for God's attributes like love, power, wisdom, and justice do not change. (Mal. 3:6) If God simply forgave indiscriminately, there would be no reason to respect him and his laws or love him to the point of fearing to displease him. The provision that the Father made was his only-begotten Son, Jesus Christ. Paul wrote,

"For all have sinned and fall short of the glory of God, and are justified by his grace as a gift, through the redemption that is in Christ Jesus, whom God put forward as a propitiation by his blood, to be received by faith. This was to show God's righteousness, because in his divine forbearance he had passed over former sins. It was to show his righteousness at the present time, so that he might be just and the justifier of the one who has faith in Jesus." – Romans 3:23-26, ESV.

Lastly, we need to understand the issues that were raised in the Garden of Eden and those brought out during Satan and God's discussion over Job. God allowing sin to enter into the world for a time has settled these issues. When people ask about why God allows pain and suffering, these issues that were raised are the answer as to why.[98] – Genesis 2:17; 3:1-6; Job 1:6-11; 2:4-5.

The Issues at Hand

(1) Satan called God a liar and said he was not to be trusted, as to the life or death issue.

(2) Satan's challenge, therefore, took into question the right and legitimacy of God's rightful place as the Universal Sovereign.

(3) Satan also suggested that people would remain obedient to God only as long as their submitting to God was to their benefit.

(4) Satan all but said that humankind was able to walk on his own, there being no need for dependence on God.

(5) Satan argued that man could be like God, choosing for himself what is right and wrong.

(6) Satan claimed that God's way of ruling was not in the best interests of humans, and they could do better without God.

True Repentance

For more than 1,500 years, there were "times of ignorance God overlooked, but now he commands all people everywhere to repent, because he has fixed a day on which he will judge the world in righteousness by a man whom he has appointed; and of this he has given assurance to all by raising him from the dead." (Ac 17:30-31, ESV) The apostle Peter tells us, "The Lord is not slow to fulfill his promise as some

---

[98] **Suffering & Evil - Why God?**

http://www.christianpublishers.org/suffering-evil-why-god

count slowness, but is patient toward you, not wishing that any should perish, but that all should reach repentance." – 2 Peter 3:9, ESV.

The apostle Paul tells us, "Without faith it is impossible to please him, for whoever would draw near to God must believe that he exists and that he rewards those who seek him." (Heb. 11:6, ESV) The prophet Micah informs us as well when he writes, "He has told you, O man, what is good; and what does the Lord require of you but to do justice, and to love kindness, and to walk humbly with your God?" For us in our imperfection to approach God and find ourselves in a righteous standing before him, we must repent and turnaround from our former ways. As we draw closer to God and learn of his righteous requirements, we must fully understand our sinful condition as was mentioned above and be aware of our spiritual needs. – Luke 18:13; Ezra 9:3-15; Matt. 26:75.

The apostle John says, "If we confess our sins, he is faithful and just to forgive us our sins and to cleanse us from all unrighteousness." (1 John 1:9) He goes on to say, "My little children, I am writing these things to you so that you may not commit a sin.[99] But if anyone does sin, we have an advocate with the Father, Jesus Christ the righteous one." (1 John 2:1) Jesus is "the Lamb of God who takes away the sin of the world!" – John 1:29. If we are truly repentant, there will be godly sorrow, based on our love for God and our love of his attributes like justice, righteousness, not simply because we are afraid that we will be punished otherwise. Paul tells us, "For godly grief produces a repentance that leads to salvation without regret, whereas worldly grief produces death." (2 Cor. 7:10, ESV) In fact, it is 'God's kindness that is meant to lead us to repentance.' – Romans 2:4.

Fruit Worthy of Repentance

To those Jews who traveled out to see John the Baptist, the man who prepared the way for Jesus Christ, he said, "produce fruit worthy of repentance!" (Lu 3:8, LEB) As James tells us, "the body apart from the spirit is dead, so also faith apart from works is dead." (Jam 2:26, ESV) What are the fruits that are "worthy of repentance"?

The apostle Peter gives us the first fruit, "Repent therefore, and turn back, that your sins may be blotted out." (Ac 3:19, ESV) "This refers to a change of mind and purpose that turns an individual from sin to God (1

---

[99] Gr., *hamartete,* a verb in the aorist subjunctive. According to *A Grammar of New Testament Greek,* by James H. Moulton, Vol. I, 1908, p. 109, "the Aorist has a 'punctiliar' action, that is, it regards action as a *point:* it represents the point of entrance . . . or that of completion . . . or it looks at a whole action simply as having occurred, without distinguishing any steps in its progress."

Thess. 1:9). Such change involves more than fearing the consequences of God's judgment. Genuine repentance knows that the evil of sin must be forsaken and the person and work of Christ totally and singularly embraced. Peter exhorted his hearers to repent, otherwise they would not experience true conversion (see note on Matt. 3:2; cf. 3:19; 5:31; 8:22; 11:18; 17:30; 20:21; 26:20; Matt. 4:17)."[100] After we have repented and turned ourselves back, we are to "live for the rest of the time in the flesh no longer for human passions but for the will of God." (1 Pet. 4:2, ESV) Yes, the fruitage of repentance demands that we dedicate ourselves to doing the will of the Father and following in the footsteps of the Son, Jesus Christ. The first step that a new one would follow would to make a public display of his or her dedication to God, by being baptized.

One major fruit of repentance is our proclaiming the good news to others. If we do not witness about God's Word, our repentance would be meaningless. Paul wrote, "For with the heart one believes and is justified, and with the mouth one confesses and is saved." (Rom. 10:10) MacArthur writes, "**confession**. This Greek word basically means to say the same thing, or to be in agreement with someone. The person who confesses Jesus as Lord (v. 9) agrees with the Father's declaration that Jesus is Savior and Lord." (MacArthur, The MacArthur Bible Commentary 2005, L. 52254-5)

If we are going to have works that befit repentance, we must no longer practice any sin, i.e., live in sin. Peter writes of our former course of conduct, "For the time that is past suffices for doing what the Gentiles want to do, living in sensuality, passions, drunkenness, orgies, drinking parties, and lawless idolatry. 4 With respect to this they are surprised when you do not join them in the same flood of debauchery, and they malign you." (1 Pet 4:3, ESV) Rather we are to carry on "the fruit of the Spirit, [which] is love, joy, peace, patience, kindness, goodness, faithfulness, gentleness, self-control; against such things there is no law." – Galatians 5:22-23.

If we are demonstrating fruitage of repentance, we must "also have forgiven our debtors." Jesus said to Peter who thought forgiving seven times was enough, "I do not say to you seven times, but seventy-seven times." – Matthew 6:12; 18:22, ESV.

However, we need to understand that we are sinners, living in imperfection, so we are not going to go through life never sinning again. Thus, while we should feel the appropriate measure of remorse when we fall short, depending on the sin (say lying versus adultery), we should not be grieved to a state of irrational thinking (i.e., "I am worthless," "I am no good, etc.). Remember our previous chapter and John's words, "But if we

---

[100] MacArthur, John (2005-05-09). *The MacArthur Bible Commentary* (Kindle Locations 49041-49044). Thomas Nelson. Kindle Edition.

walk in the light, as he is in the light, we have fellowship with one another, and the blood of Jesus his Son cleanses us from all sin." (1 John 1:7, ESV) We need to consider how God views us after we genuinely repent from falling short. "Blessed is the one whose transgression is forgiven, whose sin is covered." (Psa. 32:1, ESV) When we consider all that is involved in fruitages of repentance, we can be certain that there is no such thing as deathbed repentance. Hollywood movies and television shows are famous with Catholic priests who absolve people of their sins on their deathbed. First, only Jesus Christ can forgive sin. Second, there is no way one can store up treasures in heaven by fruitage to God and compliance with Christ's commands, and last-minute regrets cannot ransom anyone. It is like the criminal that enjoyed his crime spree until he is caught and now he regrets his actions. For some, there attempts at deathbed repentance will come at Armageddon, where they will realize that God is real, and they have missed the opportunity at eternal life.

If we are in the Christian faith, we need to spend time building up our faith, not becoming complacent. We do this by having a regular prayer life. (Phil. 4:6; Col. 4:2) It is imperative that we have a daily personal Bible study and a weekly family study if we have a family. (Matt. 4:4; 2 Tim. 3:17) We need also to prepare for all of our Christian meetings, to participate and build others up. (1 Cor. 12:12-27; Heb. 10:23-25) If there are any who are truly Christian, finding that they are overtaken in gross sin, they should quickly repent of their wrong conduct. They should go to God in prayer first, and then to those taking the lead in the congregation.

First to God and then to the responsible ones in His visible organization he should make open confession of his wrong, express his repentance and earnestly seek forgiveness, expressing their godly sorrow.

Review Questions

- What is repentance, how does it differ from the OT to the NT and just how significant is it?

- What are the truth and principles in biblical repentance?

- What is sin and how did it enter into humanity?

- What is the extent of our inherited imperfection?

- What issues have been raised by Satan that needed to be settled?

- What is true repentance?

- What are some fruitages of repentance?

CHAPTER 10 You Must Fight the Good Fight

2 Timothy 4:7 Updated American Standard Version (UASV)

⁷ I have fought the good fight,[101] I have finished the course, I have kept the faith;

Imagine a soldier in the Iraq or Afghanistan war over the past 14 years being given the command: "Head home and spend some time with your family." Most would be overjoyed at such an opportunity.

Well, we have an example of this in Scripture, where King David of Israel ordered, Uriah one of his foreign warriors, to return home, where his young, beautiful wife, Bathsheba, awaited him. Yes, it is true that King David had slept with Bathsheba, committing adultery, and impregnated her, so he wanted Uriah to have relations so that he would believe it was his child. Setting aside David's serious sin, we must note Uriah was unaware of all of this that was playing out behind the scenes. Therefore, we note Uriah repeatedly refused to go to his house. He was eventually asked why? Uriah replied, "The ark and Israel and Judah dwell in booths, and my lord Joab and the servants of my lord are camping in the open field. Shall I then go to my house, to eat and to drink and to lie with my wife? As you live, and as your soul lives, I will not do this thing." – 2 Samuel 11:8-11, ESV.

The conduct of Uriah is important to us because those who are truly Christian are presently facing a time of war as well. Are we going to be more focused on family, friends, our station in life, wealth, or are we going to seek first the kingdom of God overwhelmingly. We are in a war that has been raging for 2,000 years and looks to be entering critical times that will be very hard to deal with, unlike anything we humanity has every experience before, and it will only go from bad to worse. The signs that Jesus gave in Matthew chapter 24, Mark chapter 13 and Luke chapter 21 were to lead into "a great tribulation, such as has not occurred since the beginning of the world until now, nor ever will." (Matt. 24:21, NASB) Of course, at the culmination of the great tribulation is Jesus return with his

---

[101] "The form of the three Greek verbs 'have fought, have finished, have kept,' indicate completed action with continuing results. Paul saw his life as complete. He had been able to accomplish, through the Lord's power, all that God called him to do. He was a soldier (2:3, 4; 2 Cor. 10:3; 1 Tim. 6:12; Philem. 2), an athlete (1 Cor. 9:24–27; Eph. 6:12), and a guardian (1:13, 14; 1 Tim. 6:20, 21). the faith. The truths and standards of the revealed Word of God." – MacArthur, John (2005-05-09). *The MacArthur Bible Commentary* (Kindle Locations 60887-60890). Thomas Nelson. Kindle Edition.

angelic army at the war of Armageddon. Whether this is a year away, five years, or fifty years, we do not know.

No One Knows That Day and Hour

Matthew 24:36 English Standard Version (ESV)

[36] "But concerning that day and hour no one knows, not even the angels of heaven, nor the Son, but the Father only.

While none of us can know the precise time of Jesus' return, we do know that we are to be busy in the work that he has given us. Regardless of the time left, how will you use it? Here is how we should use our time before Christ's return. We should **live as though it is tomorrow,** but **plan as though it is 50-years away.** What do we mean by this? We **live as though** Christ is returning tomorrow, by walking with God, having a righteous standing before him. We **plan as though** it is 50-years away by living a life that has strategies for a long-term evangelism that fulfills our end of the great commission. – Matthew 24:14; 28:19-20; Acts 1:8.

Our sinful nature would not do well if we knew the exact day and hour. We do badly enough when we simply think Christ's return is close. You have had religions that have set dates for Christ's return, or are constantly saying, 'the end is near!' The ones who set actual dates for Christ's return: quit their jobs, sell their homes, take all their money out of the bank, and take their kids out of school, either (1) to have a good time before the end, or (2) to spend the last couple years yelling from the rooftops that "the end is coming!"

Those who are constantly saying, 'the end is near,' are similar, in that they do not take job promotions because it would cut into their evangelism, they do not allow their children to have university educations or plan careers, because to them the end is near. Nevertheless, these groups are at least concerned about their evangelism but fail to realize; we do not know when the end is coming. We do know one thing about the end as it draws near. We know that true Christians and Christian will be under critical unlike anything ever experienced in the past, and it will only worsen as the end closes in on us. We will talk more on this in a moment.

We need to find a way in the time that remains, be it 5 years or 50 years, to encourage and foster "sincere brotherly love," and to display "obedience to the truth." What do we need to be obedient to? (1) We need to clean up the household of Christianity. (2) We need to then, carry out the great commission that Jesus assigned, to preach, to teach, and to make disciples! (Matt 24:14; 28:19-20; Ac 1:8) It is our assignment, in the time remaining, to assist God in helping those with a receptive heart, to accept the good news of the kingdom. Yes, we are offering those of the world, the hope of getting on the path of salvation, an opportunity at everlasting life. Just because we do not know the day or the hour, does not mean that we should be less urgent about this assignment. Remember Jesus' illustration,

Matthew 24:43 English Standard Version (ESV)

[43] But know this, that if the master of the house had known in what part of the night the thief was coming, he would have stayed awake and would not have let his house be broken into.

Moreover, remember Jesus' question,

Luke 18:8 English Standard Version (ESV)

[8] I tell you, he will give justice to them speedily. Nevertheless, when the Son of Man comes, will he find faith on earth?"

The Christian War

The Christian war that has now entered a new era of difficulties will grow increasingly hostile, of which all true Christians are involved, and must endure to the end. The risks and dangers are great, and the enemy is formidable. In the Christian war, no shots are fired by some Christian military, no bombs will be dropped on our enemies, but our war strategy will be no less intense.

In any earthly war, one must know what is morally right and what is being fought for before taking up arms against another country. Is the end goal worth the casualties suffered: lives, money, and property? We need to ask ourselves the same questions before entering this Christian war. The apostle Paul tells us, "Fight the good fight of the faith." Yes, our war is not to protect the United States of America or some physical property, but rather "the faith," i.e., the Biblical truths revealed in the Word of God. If we are going to give our lives for "the faith," that is these 'truths,' there must be no doubt, if we intend to finish the course. – 1 Timothy 6:12, ESV.

A wise, careful, cautious, farsighted warrior will know the enemy he faces. The enemy we Christians face are liberal, atheistic governments, radical Islam, but even more dangerous, a superhuman being. This enemy is invisible to the eye, having superior intellect, with thousands of years of fighting experience, possessing millions of other superhuman soldiers, with superior weapons. This enemy knows every word that we have ever uttered, every action we have ever taken, which allows him to strategize just how to take us out. He is malicious, ferocious and powerful, and wicked and deceitful; he is Satan. The apostle Peter warns us, "be on the alert. Your adversary, the devil, prowls around like a roaring lion, seeking someone to devour." (1 Pet 5:8, NASB) There is not one human weapon that can be used against this enemy, nor will human cunning and trickery have any impact on this opponent. (2 Cor. 10:4) What can Christians use to wage war against such an adversary?

The Whole Armor of God

Ephesians 6:10-19 Updated American Standard Version (UASV)

[10] Finally, be strong in the Lord and in the strength of His might. [11] Put on the full armor of God, so that you will be able to stand firm against the schemes of the devil. [12] For our struggle[102] is not against flesh and blood, but against the rulers, against the powers, against the world-rulers of this darkness, against the wicked spirit forces in the heavenly places.

[13] Therefore, take up the whole armor of God, so that you will be able to resist in the evil day, and having done everything, to stand firm. [14] Stand firm, therefore, with your **loins girded**[103] about with truth, and having put on the **breastplate of righteousness**, [15] and with your **feet shod** with the preparation of the gospel of peace; [16] in all things, taking up the **shield of faith** with which you will be able to extinguish all the flaming arrows of the evil one. [17] And take the **helmet of salvation**, and the sword of the Spirit, which is the word of God.

[18] Through all prayer and petition praying at all times in the Spirit, and with this in view, keep awake with all perseverance and making supplication for all the holy ones. [19] Pray also for me, that the words may be given to me when I open my mouth, so that I may be able to speak boldly in making known the mystery of the gospel, [20] for which I am an ambassador in chains;[104] that in it I may speak boldly, as I ought to speak.

You may be thinking that it seems very unlikely that any human can be at odds with a demonic spirit creature, and come out victorious as they have unimaginable superhuman abilities. It is only possible by our reliance on Christ Jesus. We must have a complete grasp of God's Word, and apply it in a balanced manner in our lives each day. Only by doing so, can we be freed from the bodily, moral, emotional and mental harm that those under demonic or satanic control have gone through. Only by doing so may we compete with the human element that Satan will use against us as well. – Ephesians 6:11; James 4:7.

---

[102] Lit., "wrestling."

[103] (an idiom, literally 'to gird up the loins') to cause oneself to be in a state of readiness–'to get ready, to prepare oneself.'–GELNTBSD

[104] Lit *a chain*

Defending the Loins, the Breast, and the Feet

Girding Your Loins with Truth

The loins are the area on each side of the backbone of a human between the ribs and hips. At the time that the apostle Paul wrote this to the Ephesians, soldiers wore a belt or girdle-like you see in the image of Roman soldiers. It was 2 to 6 inches in width. This belt served a double duty: (1) to protect the soldier's loins, (2) but it also serves in supporting his sword. When a soldier girded up his loins, this meant he was getting ready to go into battle. This soldier and his belt served as the perfect analogy, of how a Christian is to put on the belt of biblical truth, to protect his life. The truths of Scripture should be pulled tight around us, helping us to live a life that is reflective of that truth. Thus, we can use that Bible truth to defend the faith, contend for the faith, and save those who doubt. (1 Pet. 3:15, Jude 3, 21-22) If we are to accomplish these tasks, we will have to study the Bible carefully and consider its contents. Prophetically, it was said of Jesus, "your law is within my heart." (Ps. 40:8) If Jesus came under attack by the enemy of truth, he was able to refer to biblical truth from memory. – Matthew 19:3-6; 22:23-32.

Isaiah 30:20-21 Updated American Standard Version (UASV)

20 And though Jehovah[105] give you the bread of distress and the water of oppression, yet your Teacher[106] will no longer hide himself, but your eyes shall behold your Teacher. 21 And your ears shall hear a word behind you, saying, "This is the way, walk in it," when you turn to the right or when you turn to the left.

> **Stand therefore.** For the third time (see vv. 11, 13), the apostle calls Christians to take a firm position in the spiritual battle against Satan and his minions. Whether confronting Satan's efforts to distrust God, forsaking obedience, producing doctrinal confusion and falsehood, hindering service to God, bringing division, serving God in the flesh, living hypocritically, being worldly, or in any other way rejecting biblical obedience, this armor is our defense. girded . . . with truth. The soldier wore a tunic of loose-fitting cloth. Since ancient combat was largely hand-to-hand, a loose tunic was a potential hindrance and danger. A belt was necessary to cinch up the loosely hanging material. Cf. Exodus 12:11; Luke 12:35; 1 Peter 1:13. Girding up was a matter of pulling in the loose ends as preparation for battle.

---

[105] One of 134 scribal changes from *YHWH* to *Adhonai*.

[106] Lit *your teachers*. The Hebrew verb is plural to denote grandeur or excellence.

The belt that pulls all the spiritual loose ends in is "truth" or better, "truthfulness." The idea is of sincere commitment to fight and win without hypocrisy—self-discipline in devotion to victory. Everything that hinders is tucked away. Cf. 2 Timothy 2:4; Hebrews 12:1.[107]

Breastplate of Righteousness

The breastplate of the soldier was a piece of armor that covered the chest, protecting one of the most important organs, the heart. As all Christians likely know, we have a figurative heart, which is our inner person, and it needs special protection because it leans toward wrongdoing. (Gen. 8:21) Therefore, we must cultivate a love for God's Word and the standards and values that lie within. (Ps. 119:97, 105) Our love for the Word of God should be to such a depth that we would reject "the desires of the flesh and the desires of the eyes and pride of life." (1 Jn. 2:15-17) In addition, once we have developed such a desire for right over wrong, we will be able to avoid paths that would have otherwise led us to a ruination. (Ps. 119:99-101; Am. 5:15) Our greatest example in everything, Jesus Christ, evidenced this to such an extent that Paul could say, "You have loved righteousness and hated wickedness."–Hebrews 1:9.

> the breastplate of righteousness. The breastplate was usually a tough, sleeveless piece of leather or heavy material with animal horn or hoof pieces sewn on, covering the soldier's full torso, protecting his heart and other vital organs. Because righteousness, or holiness, is such a distinctive characteristic of God Himself, it is not hard to understand why that is the Christian's chief protection against Satan and his schemes. As believers faithfully live in obedience to and communion with Jesus Christ, His own righteousness produces in them the practical, daily righteousness that becomes their spiritual breastplate. Lack of holiness, on the other hand, leaves them vulnerable to the great enemy of their souls (cf. Is. 59:17; 2 Cor. 7:1; 1 Thess. 5:8).[108]

Shod Your Feet with the Preparation of the Gospel of Peace

Roman soldiers needed suitable footwear, which (1) kept their footing sure in battle, and (2) allowed them to march some 20 miles during a campaign while wearing or carrying some 60 pounds of armor and equipment. Thus, Paul's ongoing analogy of the armor of a Roman soldier was right on target, as the appropriate footwear for the readiness of a

---

[107] MacArthur, John (2005-05-09). *The MacArthur Bible Commentary* (Kindle Locations 57513-57520). Thomas Nelson. Kindle Edition.

[108] IBID

Christian minister active in spreading the gospel message is even more important. Paul shows the importance again in his letters to the Roman congregation. There he asks how the people will get to know God if the Christian is not willing and ready to bring it to him, as he preaches and teaches?–Romans 10:13-15.

Once again, we must look to our example Jesus Christ, as he says to the Roman Governor Pontius Pilate, "For this purpose I was born and for this purpose I have come into the world, to bear witness to the truth. Everyone who is of the truth listens to my voice." For three and a half years, Jesus walked throughout the land of Palestine, preaching to all who would listen, giving the ministry top priority in his life. (John 4:5-34; 18:37) If we, like Jesus, are eager to declare the good news, we will find many opportunities to share it with others. Furthermore, our being absorbed in our ministry will help keep us spiritually strong. – Acts 18:5.

> **shod . . . with . . . the gospel of peace.** Roman soldiers wore boots with nails in them to grip the ground in combat. The gospel of peace pertains to the good news that, through Christ, believers are at peace with God and He is on their side (Rom. 5:6–10). It is that confidence of divine support which allows the believer to stand firm, knowing that he is at peace with God and God is his strength (see Rom. 8:31, 37–39).[109]

The Shield of Faith, the Helmet of Salvation, and the Sword of the Spirit

Thureon is the Greek word rendered "shield," which actually refers to a shield that was "large and oblong, protecting every part of the soldier; the word is used metaphorically of faith."[110] This shield of faith would and will protect the Christian from the "the fiery darts of the evil one." In ancient times, the darts[111] of the soldiers were often hollowed out having small iron receptacles, which were filled with a clear colorless flammable mixture of light hydrocarbons that burned. This was one of the most lethal weapons as it caused havoc among the enemy troops, unless the soldiers had the large body shields that had been drenched in water and could quench the fiery darts. In fact, the earliest manuscripts repeat the definite

---

[109] IBID

[110] W. E. Vine, Merrill F. Unger and William White, Jr., vol. 2, Vine's Complete Expository Dictionary of Old and New Testament Words (Nashville, TN: T. Nelson, 1996), 571.

[111] 6.36 belos, ous n: a missile, including arrows (propelled by a bow) or darts (hurled by hand)—'arrow, dart.' In the NT belos occurs only in a highly figurative context, to bele ... peporomena 'flaming arrows (or darts)' Eph 6:16, and refers to temptations by the Devil.—Louw and Nida 6.36.

article, literally "the darts of the evil one, the fiery (darts)," emphasizing the fact that they were above all destructive. If the soldier's shield caught fire, he would be tempted to throw it down, leaving himself open to the enemy's spear.

What does the highly metaphorical language of the fiery darts depict and how does this weaken or undercut our faith? It may come in the form of minor persecution if we live in the Western world, such as being ridiculed for our Christian faith, even verbally assaulted by Bible critics. Another fiery dart may be the temptation to put money over the ministry. Then, there is the constant temptation from Satan's world to lure us into immorality. You would have to be literally blindfolded not to see sexually explicit images hundreds of times per day, as it is used to sell everything. It is not only the images but also the mindset. I will give you just one example, and please excuse the graphic nature. The modern-day junior high school children (13 and 14 years old); literally view oral sex as being no different than kissing one another on the lips.

If we are to protect our Christian family, our congregation of brothers and sisters, and ourselves, we must possess **"the shield of faith."** Faith is not a simple belief in Jesus Christ as some misinformed ones might tell us; rather it is an active faith in Jesus Christ. James tells at 1:19 "You believe that God is one; you do well. Even the demons believe, and shudder!" The demons and Satan believe in the existence of Jesus Christ, and yet this brings them no salvation whatsoever. Faith comes from taking in an active knowledge of the Father and the Son to the point of building a relationship, a friendship based on the deepest love, and the committing of oneself to the point of turning your life over completely. It is regular prayerful communication, understanding and valuing how he protects us. – Joshua 23:14; Luke 17:5; Romans 10:17.

Yet again, we turn to our great exemplar, Jesus Christ, who demonstrated his faith throughout some very trying times. He completely trusted the Father to accomplish his will and purposes. (Matthew 26:42, 53, 54; John 6:38) A great example of this trust can be found when Jesus was in the garden of Gethsemane. He was in great anguish because he knew that he was going to be executed as a blasphemer of his Father, and even then, he fell with his face to the ground and prayed, "My Father, if it is possible, may this cup be taken from me. Yet not as I will, but as you will." (Matthew 26:39) Not that he was backing out of the execution, the ransom that is, but he wanted to be executed for another reason, other than a blasphemer. Jesus was an integrity keeper, which brought great joy to the Father. (Proverbs 27:11) As we face difficult times in the world that is alienated from God, we will do well to imitate Jesus great faith, and not give our under the pressures of a world that lies in the hands of the evil one. Moreover, our faith will be refined if we trust in God, evidencing our love for him, by applying his Word in our daily walking with him. (Psalm 19:7-11; 1 John 5:3) The immediate gratifications that this world has to offer could never compare with the blessings that lie ahead. – Proverbs 10:22.

6:16 the shield of faith. This Greek word usually refers to the large shield (2.5 ft. x 4.5 ft.) that protected the entire body. The faith to which Paul refers is not the body of Christian doctrine (as the term is used in 4:13) but basic trust in God. The believer's continual trust in God's word and promise is "above all" absolutely necessary to protect him from temptations to every sort of sin. All sin comes when the victim falls to Satan's lies and promises of pleasure, rejecting the better choice of obedience and blessing. **fiery darts.** Temptations are likened to the flaming arrows shot by the enemy and quenched by the oil-treated leather shield (cf. Ps. 18:30; Prov. 30:5, 6; 1 John 5:4).[112]

Not long ago, those trying to curb the use of drugs within the American youth had the saying, "the mind is a terrible thing to waste." Our next piece of armor of God would be a very useful tool for protecting the Christian mind, **the helmet of salvation.** The Apostle Paul said to the Thessalonians, "we must stay sober and let our faith and love be like a suit of armor. Our firm hope that we will be saved is our helmet," because it protects our Christian mind. (1 Thessalonians 5:8) Even though we may have accepted Christ, and have entered onto the path of salvation, we still suffer from imperfect human weaknesses. Even though our foremost desire is to do good, our thinking can be corrupted by this fleshly world that surrounds us. We need to **not** be like this world, but rather openly allow God to alter the way we think, through his Word the Bible, which will help us fully to grasp everything that is good and pleasing to him. (Romans 7:18; 12:2) You likely recall the test that Jesus faced, where Satan offered him "all the kingdoms of the world and their glory." (Matthew 4:8-10) Jesus response was to refer to Scripture, "Be gone, Satan! For it is written, 'you shall worship the Lord your God and him only shall you serve.'" Paul had this to say about Jesus, "looking to Jesus, the founder and perfecter of our faith, who for the joy that was set before him endured the cross, despising the shame, and is seated at the right hand of the throne of God." – Hebrews 12:2.

We need to understand that the above examples of faith, does not come to us automatically. If we focusing on what this current system of things has to offer, as opposed to focusing on the hopes that are plainly laid out in Scripture, we will be weak in the face of any difficult trial. After

---

[112] IBID

a few stumbles, it may be that we suffer spiritual shipwreck and lose our hope altogether. Then again, if we frequently feed our minds, or concentrate the mind on the promises of God, we will carry on delighting in the hope that has been offered us. Romans 12:12.

6:17 the helmet of salvation. The helmet protected the head, always a major target in battle. Paul is speaking to those who are already saved, and is therefore not speaking here about attaining salvation. Rather, Satan seeks to destroy a believer's assurance of salvation with his weapons of doubt and discouragement. This is clear from Paul's reference to "a helmet the hope of salvation" (Is. 59:17; see note on 1 Thess. 5:8). But although a Christian's feelings about his salvation may be seriously damaged by Satan-inspired doubt, his salvation itself is eternally protected and he need not fear its loss. Satan wants to curse the believer with doubts, but the Christian can be strong in God's promises of eternal salvation in Scripture (see John 6:37–39; 10:28, 29; Rom. 5:10; 8:31–39; Phil. 1:6; 1 Pet. 1:3–5). Security is a fact; assurance is a feeling that comes to the obedient Christian (1 Pet. 1:3–10).[113]

If we are to keep our Christian mind on the hope that lies ahead, we need to possess **the Sword of the Spirit**.[114] The loving letter from our heavenly Father, his Word, the Bible is stated to be "living and active, sharper than any two-edged sword, piercing to the division of soul and of spirit, of joints and of marrow, and discerning the thoughts and intentions of the heart." This Word, if understood correctly, applied in a balanced manner, can transform our lives, and help us avoid or minimalize the pitfalls of this imperfect life. We can depend on that Word when we are overwhelmed, or temple to give way to the flesh, and when the Bible critics of this world attempt to do away with our faith. (2 Corinthians 10:4-5) We need to heed the words of the Apostle Paul to his spiritual son, Timothy:

2 Timothy 3:14-17 Updated American Standard Version (UASV)

[14] You **[Timothy]**, however, continue in the things you have learned and were persuaded to believe, knowing from whom you have learned them **[Paul, who Timothy traveled with and studied under for 15 years]**, [15]

---

[113] IBID

[114] **the sword of the Spirit**. As the sword was the soldier's only weapon, so God's Word is the only needed weapon, infinitely more powerful than any of Satan's. The Greek term refers to a small weapon (6–18 in. long). It was used both defensively to fend off Satan's attacks, and offensively to help destroy the enemy's strategies. It is the truth of Scripture. – IBID

and that from infancy[115] you have known the sacred writings **[the whole Old Testament]**, which are able to make you wise for salvation through trust[116] in Christ Jesus. [16] All Scripture is inspired by God and profitable for teaching, for reproof, for correction, for training in righteousness; [17] so that the man of God may be fully competent, equipped for every good work.

On these verses, New Testament Bible scholar Knute Larson writes,

> **3:14–15.** Each of us is susceptible to this dangerous trap of deception unless we obey Scripture vigilantly. Following Christ is more than a one-time decision or an occasional church service or kind act. True Christianity involves continual dependence and obedience to Christ the king. Paul told Timothy to **continue in what you have learned and have become convinced of.** Our faith is proved by its endurance.
>
> Two elements are necessary for faithful living. First, we must possess knowledge of the truth. Truth enlightens a person about what is right and wrong, what constitutes purpose and happiness. We cannot trust or love which we do not know. The second element is conviction or belief. We express our belief system in the daily decisions we make and the behaviors in which we engage. No one acts contrary to belief (though we may act contrary to our professions of belief).
>
> Paul also wanted Timothy to consider **those from whom you learned [truth], and how from infancy you have known the holy Scriptures.** Once again he had Timothy's mother and grandmother in mind (see 2 Tim. 1:5). Timothy was schooled in the Old Testament writings and had learned the need for forgiveness, the provision of God, and the necessity of faith. He had also been discipled by Paul, learning Christ and the church. In each case, Timothy had not only been given knowledge; he had been witness to godly lives.
>
> These people served as examples to Timothy about the truth of God, the need for endurance, and the reward of faithfulness. Each person had staked his or her life on the revelation of the Scriptures which, according to Paul, **are able to make you wise for salvation through faith in Christ Jesus.** (Larson 2000, 306)

---

[115] *Brephos* is "the period of time when one is very young–'childhood (probably implying a time when a child is still nursing), infancy." – GELNTBSD

[116] *Pisteuo* is "to believe to the extent of complete trust and reliance—'to believe in, to have confidence in, to have faith in, to trust, faith, trust.' – GELNTBSD

The apostle Paul stressed the significance of God's Word when he wrote to Timothy, "Continue in what you have learned and have firmly believed." "The things" that Paul revealed are Bible truths, which moved Timothy to grow into having faith in the gospel. These same truths, along with the entire Word of God (i.e., "All Scripture), can affect us today in the same way, making us "wise for salvation through faith in Christ Jesus."

Enemy Strategies

To fight with, struggle against, or deal with the world of mankind alienated from God or Satan and his demons is like walking through a field sown with landmines. An attack against our faith can come from any quarter, and our enemies try to catch us by surprise. However, rest assured, "No temptation has overtaken you that is not common to man. God is faithful, and he will not let you be tempted beyond your ability, but with the temptation, he will also provide the way of escape, that you may be able to endure it." – 1 Corinthians 10:13.

The most straightforward **attack** the past thirty years has been **against Bible truths that are fundamental to our faith.** The problem is that Christianity was slow to respond to the threat. For a time the atheist and agnostic was penning books written on a layman's level, while Bible scholars were busy penning academic books that the average churchgoer would have no interest. The modern day Bible critic is better prepared as well because he has been devouring the Bible critic books.[117] Christians on the other have been caught unawares because they do not devour Christian apologetic books with the same vigor.[118] The Bible critics use smooth words

---

[117] HERE ARE A FEW BOOK BY THE BIBLE CRITIC

The God Delusion by Richard Dawkins

Why There Is No God: Simple Responses to 20 Common Arguments for the Existence of God by Armin Navabi and Nicki Hise

God Is Not Great: How Religion Poisons Everything by Christopher Hitchens

Misquoting Jesus: The Story Behind Who Changed the Bible and Why by Bart D. Ehrman

[118] HERE ARE A FEW BOOK BY CHRISTIAN APOLOGISTS

MISREPRESENTING JESUS: Debunking Bart D. Ehrman's "Misquoting Jesus" [Third Edition] by Edward D. Andrews

Misquoting Truth: A Guide to the Fallacies of Bart Ehrman's "Misquoting Jesus" by Timothy Paul Jones

Defending Your Faith: An Introduction to Apologetics by R. C. Sproul

Holman QuickSource Guide to Christian Apologetics (Holman Quicksource Guides)

and twisted words, misrepresenting the facts, in an effort to cause spiritual shipwreck. Proverbs 11:9 notes, "With his mouth the godless man would destroy his neighbor, but by knowledge the righteous are delivered."

It would be a mistake to tell Christians to not read books by Bible critics; this gives the impression that you are hiding something from them. The better approach would be to have the Christian read a few Christian apologetic books, opening their eyes, and then have them read the Bible critic books. This way, with the knowledge they took in they will be able to identify the lies, the misleading, and the misrepresenting of the Bible critic.

Another tool of Satan is **entertainment**. Another measure that needs to be taken is the fleeing from anything that will generate wrong desires, which lead to wrong actions. This means keeping our eyes and ears away from pornography and homosexual advocates. (Col. 3:5) We need to understand that the Bible's moral values are not respected in today's world.

Parents, teachers, couches, and the like influenced the youth of the 1950s and 1960s. Most young people today are very much influenced by hip-hop, rap, and heavy metal music, as well reality television, celebrities, movies, video games, and the Internet, especially social media. Parents are now allowing their children to receive life-altering opinions, beliefs, and worldviews from the likes of Snooki, a cast member of the MTV reality show *Jersey Shore*. Kim Kardashian and her family rose to prominence with their reality television series, *Keeping Up with the Kardashians*.

The ABC Family channel (owned by Disney) comes across as a channel that you would want you children watching. However, most of the shows are nothing more than dysfunctional families, promotions of homosexuality as an alternative lifestyle, and young actors and actresses that are playing underage teens in high school, running around killing, causing havoc, and having sexual intercourse with multiple characters on the show. In August 2006, an all-new slogan and visual style premiered on ABC Family: A New Kind of Family. The channel shows such programming as Pretty Little Liars, Twisted, The Fosters, Melissa & Joey, Switched at Birth, The Lying Game, Bunheads and Baby Daddy.

The world has added new words to their vocabulary, like "sexting," which is the act of sending sexually explicit messages and/or photographs, primarily between cell phones. The term was first popularized in 2007. Then, there is "F-Bomb," which we are not going to define fully other than to say that the dictionary considers it "a lighthearted and printable

---

On Guard: Defending Your Faith with Reason and Precision by William Lane Craig and Lee Strobel

euphemism" for something far more offensive. If all of the above is unfamiliar to you as a parent, and you have a teen or preteen child, you may want to Google the information.

Regardless of the degree of the relationship, these relationships often influence the thinking of a young life. It is important that you do not allow the wrong persons to influence you or your children. The truth is our thinking, and our actions are a direct result of bad associations, be it the wrong friends, music, celebrities, video games, or social media. The same holds true of good associations, like our parents, teachers, coaches, and good friends. Paul warned, "For there are many **rebellious men, empty talkers, and deceivers**," from whom we should watch out! – Titus 1:10.

In the end, with help from God's Word, the Christian congregation, the pastor, family, and Christian counseling, you have a reasonable expectation that you will not act on the same-sex desires. Moreover, there is the possibility that you may be one of the few that begins to alter oneself to the point that the desires are no more. If not, self-control will be the way of things until God brings this wicked age to an end. The final warning offered herein is this. Do not allow charismatic religious rhetoric to suggest that the laying on of hands can heal you. This will only leave you vulnerable, as you will then let down your guard, and not seek the help that you need. What they espouse is just not how it works and is unbiblical.

Another strategy used by the enemy is the **love of money**. Paul wrote, "For the love of money is a root of all kinds of evils. It is through this craving that some have wandered away from the faith and pierced themselves with many pangs." (1 Tim. 6:10, ESV) Commenting on 1 Timothy 6:10, MacArthur writes, "Lit. "affection for silver." In the context, this sin applies to false teachers specifically, but the principle is true universally. Money itself is not evil since it is a gift from God (Deut. 8:18); Paul condemns only the love of it (cf. Matt. 6:24) which is so characteristic of false teachers (see notes on 1 Pet. 5:2; 2 Pet. 2:1–3, 15). strayed from the faith. From the body of Christian truth. Gold has replaced God for these apostates, who have turned away from pursuing the things of God in favor of money."[119]

If a soldier loses his morale, he will become an easy target for the enemy. "If you are slack [discouraged] in the day of distress, Your strength is limited." (Pro. 24:10, NASB) **Discouragement** is another strategy of Satan. The apostle Paul wrote, "But since we belong to the day, let us be sober, having put on the breastplate of faith and love, and for a helmet the hope of salvation." (1 Thess. 5:5) Wearing "a helmet the hope of salvation," will

---

[119] MacArthur, John (2005-05-09). *The MacArthur Bible Commentary* (Kindle Locations 60376-60380). Thomas Nelson. Kindle Edition.

help us fight discouragement. MacArthur writes, "Paul pictured the Christian life in military terms as being a life of soberness (alertness) and proper equipping. The breastplate covers the vital organs of the body. Faith is an essential protection against temptations because it is trust in God's promise, plan, and truth. It is an unwavering belief in God's Word that protects us from temptation's arrows. Looking at it negatively, it is unbelief that characterizes all sin. When believers sin, they have believed Satan's lie. Love for God is essential, as perfect love for Him yields perfect obedience to Him. Elsewhere, the warrior's breastplate has been used to represent righteousness (Is. 59:17; Eph. 6:14). Faith elsewhere is represented by a soldier's shield (Eph. 6:16). The helmet is always associated with salvation in its future aspects (cf. Is. 59:17; Eph. 6:17). Our future salvation is guaranteed, nothing can take it away (Rom. 13:11). Paul again combined faith, love, and hope (cf. 1:3)."[120]

Do Not Give Up the Fight

Some of us may have been fighting doubts, health problems, old age, the loss of loved ones and we may be growing weak, and, therefore, not fighting with the vigor that we once fought. Thomas D. Lea addresses the need to stay in the fight based on Hebrews 10:32-34,

> **10:32–33.** These verses urged the readers to remember the days after their conversion when they stood their ground while they faced threats to their faith. They were to remember their previous record. What a positive record it had been!

> They had refused to compromise when they faced persecution for their faith. Sometimes they had become **publicly exposed to insult and persecution.** They had endured scorn and threats from crowds. The words of 12:4 suggest that they had not yet suffered martyrdom.

> Sometimes they **stood side by side** with friends who were insulted and abused. They suffered because of their association with others. They found it a privilege to share in the sufferings of others.

> **10:34.** The general description of persecution in verse 33 becomes specific in this verse. Facing hardship involves two matters. First, they had **sympathized with those in prison.** It was common in those days for Christians to receive imprisonment for their commitment to Christ (note Paul's imprisonments mentioned in 2 Cor. 11:23). Probably at least some of the

---

[120] IBID, (Kindle Locations 59233-59240)

recipients of Hebrews had suffered imprisonment because of their Christian confession. Visiting these imprisoned believers openly identified some of the readers as Christians and made them subject to arrest and persecution. They had endured public shame because of their encouragement to imprisoned Christians.

Second, the readers had experienced the loss of their property. They took the loss with joy. They were so convinced of the truth of Christianity that they submitted joyfully to the loss of their possessions. How could they do this?

The readers had learned that in Christ they had **better and lasting possessions.** They could never lose their possessions in Christ because these possessions lasted (see Matt. 6:20). Heaven's treasures had greater appeal than the temporary blessings of earth.

As we carry on in our fight for the faith, remember Jesus' words, "These things I have spoken to you, so that in Me you may have peace. In the world you have tribulation, but take courage; I have overcome the world." (John 16:33, NASB)

Review Questions

- How does the conduct of Uriah help us?

- How should we live our lives when we do not know the day or the hour of Jesus' return?

- Who are our enemies in our Christian war? Who is the most dangerous one of them all?

- Why is it important that a soldier know his enemy?

- Explain each piece of the armor of God.

- What are the enemy's strategies?

- What may happen to the fight in us over time, and how can we get it back?

CHAPTER 11 You May Dwell with God

Is that even possible? What does it mean to dwell with Jehovah God anyway? It means that you can be God's friend. Jesus half-brother James tells us in his letter, "Abraham believed God, and it was counted to him as righteousness, and he was called a friend of God." (James 2:23, ESV) The above chapter title is figurative language that means all have the opportunity of developing such a relationship with God that he or she has access to God in prayer and worship. Let us start by meditatively reading the Psalm 15:1-5 in its entirety, and then we will do a verse-by-verse discussion of the Psalm. Read it first meticulously, emphatically hitting the ten dos and the don'ts, or conditions that give ones access to God as a friend, enabling them to approach him freely in their prayer and worship.

Psalm 15 Updated American Standard Version (UASV)

A Psalm of David.

15

O Jehovah, who may be a guest[121] in your tent?
Who shall dwell on your holy mountain?

² He **who walks blamelessly** and **does what is right**
and **speaks truth** in his heart;
³ who **does not slander** with[122] his tongue
and **does no evil** to his neighbor,
nor takes up a reproach against his friend;
⁴ in whose eyes **a vile person is despised**,
but who[123] **honors those** who fear Jehovah;
who **swears to his own hurt** and does not change;
⁵ who does **not put out his money at interest**,[124]
and does **not take a bribe** against the innocent.
He who does these things shall never be shaken.

We Walk Blamelessly and Do What is Right

The Hebrew word rendered "blameless" is *tamim*, is not a reference to a perfect condition, one without sin; it is simply living an exemplary moral life, a life that is whole or sound. When the *tamim* is used in reference to humans that live during this time of imperfection, it is meant in a relative

---

[121] Lit *sojourn*

[122] Lit *according to*

[123] Lit *he*

[124] I.e. **not** to the destitute

132

sense, not as an absolute. If we look at all of the good characteristics and qualities of the Bible, which all Christians are subject to possessing, it must be in a balanced manner. He is not expected to be perfect in all of them. He is expected to meet a certain level of competence of each, not being out of balance. He would not be kind in the extreme to others, but lack self-control in private. What does "walking" signify here? It is used in a figurative sense of following a certain course of action, life course, which is outlined in God's Word, to the extent that he finds favor in God's eyes. – Psalm 1:1; 3 John 1:3-4.

We Speak the Truth in Our Heart

How does a Christian 'speak the truth in his heart?' It means that he is consistent in what he says, he is not double hearted (Psalm 12:2), (literally, with a heart and a heart), attempting to live one way in an outward sense, while concealing another life, or deceptively saying one thing, while in his mind, he is thinking something else entirely. – 1 Chronicles 12:33

Some Christians might not out and out lie, but they speak half-truths, to avoid and discomfort that may come from telling the complete truth. Christian students cheat on their tests while their Christian parents alter the figures on their taxes to make the bottom line look better. These fall short in that they are not whole or sound when it comes to the truth. The apostle Paul said, "Do not lie to each other, since you have taken off your old self with its practices and have put on the new self, which is being renewed in knowledge in the image of its Creator." (Colossians 3:9, 10) We must ask ourselves, are we completely honest in our dealings with others? Moreover, are we completely honest with ourselves? If we are, this will affect the next condition that must be met in order to be able freely to approach God in our prayers and worship.

We Do Not Slander With Our Tongue

To slander someone is to say something false or malicious (intentionally harmful) that damages somebody's reputation. The Hebrew verb ragal is a reference to the lowest part of the leg, the body part upon which a person or animal stands, the foot (regel). It is used both literally and figuratively. It has the meaning "to foot it," in other words, "to go about." The Israelites were commanded, "You shall not go about with slander among your people." (Lev. 19:16) We are robbing a person of his good name if we slander him, deliberately trying to do harm to his or her reputation. We can help to bring slander to a halt, by refusing to listen to it, and especially not spreading it on to another. If it is of such paramount importance that we control our speech, is it not, much more important that we control what we do?

We Do No Evil to Our Neighbor

We will fare far better in life if we apply the words of Jesus, which are in harmony with Psalm 15:3: "In all things, whatever you want that people should do to you, thus also you do to them." (Matt 7:12, LEB) It is simple, we must avoid doing anything bad to other people, but it must also be a heart condition of how we feel. The Psalmist said, "O you who love Jehovah, **hate evil**: He preserves the souls of his saints; He delivers them out of the hand of the wicked."(Ps 97:10, ASV) Therefore, if we are to be a friend of God like Abraham and many other holy ones of the past, we must live by the moral standards that he created within us.

This removing of bad from our lives would fall to not doing anyone wrong when we have dealings with them. This would include what we say, as well as what we do, in our dealings with others, doing nothing to bring them any kind of harm. That is avoiding the bad, but we also need to embrace doing the good for the people that enter our lives as well. This can be as small as driving in a courteous way when we are on the road. Are we in such a hurry that we do not pause to let another driver in our lane, or out of a parking lot into traffic. We can also do good by helping the elderly, help raise the spirits of the downhearted, comfort the grieving. What does the Psalmist address next?

We Do Not Reproach Our Friends

Bringing reproach on another is criticizing him or her to another for something they may have done wrong. Each of us makes mistakes, and we would hope that our friends would overlook these small imperfect moments in our lives. It is ironic, if we make a mistake, we hope the friend ignores it and does not share it with others. However, when others are the ones that make a mistake, we can be quick to share that moment of imperfection with others. There are some in the Christian congregation, who will share minor embarrassing weaknesses of others, to sidestep their own issues, or to build themselves up, while tearing down others. However, this type of spirit does not belong to a friend of God, who throws our transgressions into the sea (so that they are so far down that they will never be seen again). One who casts our transgressions as far off as the sunrise is from the sunset (the greatest distance possible), who throws our transgressions behind his back (so he is unable to see them).--Micah 7:19; Psalm 103:12; Isaiah 38:17

Proverbs 17:9 Updated American Standard Version (UASV)

134

⁹ Whoever covers a transgression seeks love,
but he who repeats a matter separates close friends.

We are to Despise Vile Persons

A vile person is one who would have no value in the life of the true worshipers, who is unclean, lacking honesty or moral integrity, or morally corrupts. A true worshiper has to have dealings with those who practice sin in this world, but does not bond with such a person in any kind of social setting or friendship. He realizes that such an association would defile him. When a man with a white glove shakes hands with a man wearing a glove that is covered in dirt, the clean white glove does not rub off on the dirty glove; it is always the dirt coming off onto the clean glove.--1 Corinthians 5:6; 15:33

There is a tendency to overlook the defiled man if he is wealthy, famous, in a position of power. (Jude 16) We must come to the realization that friendship with God is impossible for those who become friends with those who are vile (wicked in their ways). We are to hate the wicked ones ways, anything that is contrary to the moral standard of God. (Rom. 12:9) So bad was Israel's king Jehoram that the prophet Elisha told him:

2 Kings 3:14 Updated American Standard Version (UASV)

¹⁴ And Elisha said, "As the Lord of hosts lives, before whom I stand, were it not that I have regard for Jehoshaphat the king of Judah, I would neither look at you nor see you.

If we want to be considered a friend of God, then, we will adopt his values and morals to the extent that we are uncomfortable around wrongdoers. We will have dealings only to the extent that we have to because we live in this world. As Paul said 'we must live in this world, but we need not be a part of it.' On the other hand, those we invite into our lives, as friends should be chosen based on their walk with God, not because they are wealthy, popular, or influential. We will choose our friends based on the love we have for our heavenly Father because we fear the idea of ever hurting him.

We Honor Those Who Fear God

This fear of God is not the dread that we would have of say being dangled over the edge of a cliff, or cowering in a closet as our house is being robbed by several criminals, or having a cruel employer that makes our life a living torture chamber. No, the fear of Jehovah is a reverential fear of displeasing him, because our love for him is like that of a loving father, but only greater. It is like a son, who imitates his father, so too we want to be like our heavenly Father, as we are made in his image.

Proverbs 1:7 Updated American Standard Version (UASV)

⁷ The fear of the Lord is the beginning of knowledge; fools despise wisdom and instruction.

This love for him, moves us to apply his Word more fully in our lives, it serves as a daily guide in all that we do. We realize that the values and morals that he has placed in our conscience are refined by his Word, and will help us be able to determine between what is good and what is bad. For example, one who lives by these values would apply all the Bible principles that would make him an excellent worker, meaning he would be productive, honest, and looking to be of help to all on the job site. Fellow workers may view this as attempts at seeking favor with management, looking to get ahead, so they ridicule this one. Others may feel that he is making them work harder, or look bad in the boss's eyes, so they despise him. What they do not realize is that these are his qualities as a person of God, and he has none of the evil intentions that fellow workers may suspect. Are we honoring persons like this, persons who fear God?

We Keep Our Promises Regardless of the Cost

We keep our promises that we make to Jehovah God himself, as well as to our neighbor, friends, family, employer, and so on, not allowing one word to fail, as this is what God would have done. (1 Kings 8:56; 2 Corinthians 1:20) We do this even if after having made a promise, it turns out that it is going to be more complicated, or more involved than we had originally thought. If we swear to help a neighbor one weekend and then a friend offers us a chance to go to once in a lifetime event, we keep our word. If we promise our wife that we will get something done, we get it done. Even when Joshua was tricked into giving his word to the Gibeonites, he still kept that word once he found out.

Joshua 9:16-19 Updated American Standard Version (UASV)

¹⁶ At the end of three days after they had made a covenant with them, they heard that they were their neighbors and that they lived among them.¹²⁵ ¹⁷ Then the sons of Israel set out and came to their cities on the third day. Now their cities were Gibeon and Chephirah and Beeroth and Kiriath-jearim. ¹⁸ The sons of Israel did not strike them because the leaders of the congregation had sworn to them by Jehovah the God of Israel. And the whole congregation grumbled against the leaders. ¹⁹ But all the leaders

---

¹²⁵ Or *within their land*

said to all the congregation, "We have sworn to them by Jehovah, the God of Israel, and now we cannot touch them.

Thus, if we make a commitment to another, we are obligated to that promise, and it is our integrity on the line, as well as God's good name, because when we fail to keep a promised, we bring reproach on ourselves, as well as the God that we represent. Jesus said, "Let what you say be simply 'Yes' or 'No'; anything more than this comes from evil." (Matthew 5:37) Especially should all who have dedicated their lives to Christ be ever determined to live up to their promise to be his disciple?

We Lend Our Money without Charging Interest

Of course, money lent for business purposes is an exception to this principle. David in this Psalm was referring to when we give money to those living or falling into poverty. Exodus 22:25 specifically says, "If you lend money to any of my people with you who is poor, you shall not be like a moneylender to him, and you shall not exact interest from him." We also find an account in Nehemiah where he discovered the poor being taken advantage of by others who were using them for ill-gotten gains, and he brought this to a stop.--Nehemiah 5:1-13.

As an aside, of interest is David's choice of words, for the Hebrew word he used is a derivative of another one that signifies "to bite." In other words, those greedy usurers were chewing up and devouring the destitute to line their pockets. We should rather live by the principles that Jesus outlined for us at Luke 14:12-14, "When you give a dinner or a banquet, do not invite your friends or your brothers or your relatives or rich neighbors, lest they also invite you in return, and you be repaid. But when you give a feast, invite the poor, the crippled, the lame, the blind, and you will be blessed, because they cannot repay you. For you will be repaid at the resurrection of the just." If it is our desire to be a friend of God and to dwell with him, we should never take advantage of those who are struggling financially.

We Do Not Take Bribes that Hurt the Innocent

A bribe is to give somebody money or some other incentive to do something, especially something illegal or dishonest, and this has a demeaning and shameful effect. We are told at Deuteronomy 16:19, "You shall not pervert justice. You shall not show partiality, and you shall not accept a bribe, for a bribe blinds the eyes of the wise and subverts the cause of the righteous." We are to be about just and justice alone, not perverting justice. We would never want to accept any incentive to do an innocent person wrong, which deserves justice. The greatest injustice since the fall of man had been when Judas Iscariot accepted a Bribe to betray Jesus Christ! Matthew 26:14-16.

We may believe that we are innocent under this provision, but if we have ever tried to influence another to avoid justice, in any way, we are guilty. The prophet Samuel sets the example for us to follow, "Here I am; testify against me before [Jehovah] and before his anointed. Whose ox have I taken? Or whose donkey have I taken? Or whom have I defrauded? Whom have I oppressed? Or from whose hand have I taken a bribe to blind my eyes with it? Testify against me, and I will restore it to you." They said, 'You have not defrauded us or oppressed us or taken anything from any man's hand.'" (1 Samuel 12:3, 4)

If We Do These Things We Will Stand Firm

King David closes this list of standards or criterion that we are to live by, with "he who does these things shall never be moved." The New Living Translation reads, "Such people will stand firm forever." This is not an absolute; it is relative to the imperfect condition we are in and the imperfect world in which we live. All of these kinds of statements in the Bible, if you do "A" you will get "B" are best understood if you these phrases before the statement: generally speaking, "on the whole," "by and large," or "as a rule" in the front of the verse. "Generally speaking, such people will stand firm forever." Unlike those in the world, who have their flesh as their god, we will fair far better if we do these things to the best of our Christian ability.

Of course, there is far more to being God's friend than what we have covered here in Psalm 15. Jesus brought the servant of God new spiritual light, such as what he said at John 4:23-24 "But the hour is coming and is now here, when the true worshipers will worship the Father in spirit and truth, for the Father, is seeking such people to worship him. God is spirit, and those who worship him must worship in spirit and truth." By following the Bible study program that we have outlined here in this publication, you will discover the deeper things of God, which will enable to draw closer, and become God's friend.

Review Questions

- Who are morally qualified so that may dwell with God?

- If you are to be God's friend, what must you be free of?

- Are you completely honest with yourself and others, speaking the truth in your heart?

138

- Who should we refuse to listen to?
- What does avoiding evil include?
- How does a Christian look upon upright persons?

CHAPTER 12 Walk Humbly With Your God

Micah 6:8 Updated American Standard Version (UASV)

⁸ He has told you, O mortal man, what *is* good,
and what does Jehovah require of you
but to do justice, and to love kindness,
and to walk humbly with your God?

It is certainly a difficult thing, trying to picture a puny human walk with the Creator of heaven and earth. It would be like setting a piece of sand next to the biggest bolder on earth, and this would not even be close. Of course, we are talking about a metaphorical walk, a life course that a Christian follows, one that is in harmony with Jehovah's values, will and purposes.

Others have done just that, as we learn from Scripture that "Enoch walked with God" and "Noah walked with God." If we truly are a friend of God, like Abraham, we will be living a life that is reflective of that friendship. Jehovah expects nothing less of his servants, than that they 'walk humbly with him.' – Genesis 5:22; 6:9; Malachi 2:4, 6; Micah. 6:8

If we are to walk with God in a system of things that is run by Satan, possessing a mind and body that leans naturally toward sin, it will be necessary for us to have a very close relationship, closer than any human relationship that we may have ever had. We read of Moses that it was, "by faith he left Egypt, not fearing the anger of the king, for he persevered as if he saw the invisible one." (Heb. 11:27) Even though King David had many bumps in his relationship with God, it is said that his "eyes are continually toward Jehovah." Yes, David said, "I have set Yahweh before me always. Because he is at my right hand I will not be shaken." – Psalm 25:15; 16:8, LEB.

Why should we walk with God? First, we do so because he is the giver of life, and the sovereign of the universe. Second, as our Creator, he designed us not to walk alone. How has that been working out for humanity over the past 6,000 plus years? "I know, O [Jehovah], that to the human is not his own way, nor to a person is the walking and the directing of his own step." (Jer. 10:23, LEB) Yes, we were designed to be under the umbrella of his sovereignty, possessing free will, but best served by following his lead. Therefore, our eternal happiness is dependent upon our walking with him.

We can draw comfort from the fact that God created us out of his endless love, making us in such a way, to enjoy life to the fullest extent. It was Adam who rebelled, placing us in this difficult situation. Now Jehovah is moving heaven and earth to get us back to his intended purpose. Jehovah is omniscient (all knowing), which means he knows what is best for us. Having him walk us through this difficult period in human history is the safest way to the end of this wicked system of things. – Proverbs 2:6-9; Psalm 91:1

Further, walking with God should come out of our love for him, not what we can gain from him. We should find true happiness in our friendship with him; otherwise, our motives are not pure. The Scriptures are quite clear about how he feels about our love for him, as he tells us to "Be wise, my child, and make my heart glad, and I will answer him who reproaches me with a word." – Proverbs 77:11, LEB.

Threefold Resistance

When we enter the pathway of walking with our God, we will certainly come across resistance from three different areas. **Our greatest obstacle is ourselves**, because we have inherited imperfection from our first parents Adam and Eve. The Scriptures make it quite clear that we are mentally bent toward bad, not good. (Gen 6:5; 8:21, AT) In other words, our natural desire is toward wrong. Prior to sinning, Adam and Eve were perfect, and they had the natural desire of doing good, and to go against that was to go against the grain of their inner person. Scripture also tells us of our inner person, our heart.

Jeremiah 17:9 Updated American Standard Version (UASV)

⁹ The heart is more deceitful than all else,
and desperately sick;
who can understand it?

Romans 7:21-25 Updated American Standard Version (UASV)

²¹ I find then the law in me that when I want to do right, that evil is present in me. ²² For I delight in the law of God according to the inner man, ²³ but I see a different law in my members, warring against the law of my mind and taking me captive in the law of sin which is in my members. ²⁴ Wretched man that I am! Who will deliver me from this body of death? ²⁵ Thanks be to God through Jesus Christ our Lord! So then, I myself serve the law of God with my mind, but with my flesh, I serve the law of sin.

1 Corinthians 9:27 Updated American Standard Version (UASV)

²⁷ but I discipline my body and make it my slave, so that, after I have preached to others, I myself will not be disqualified.

The **second greatest obstacle** is the **world of humankind that is alienated from God**. Its ruler, Satan, designs this world to cater to our fallen flesh. The spirit of this world comes from Satan himself, and if breathed in for too long, we will begin to adopt the same mindset, the same thinking, attitude, conduct, and speech that is opposite of Jehovah God. This poisonous air will paralyze us quite quickly if we entertain it either by thinking on it, or worse still, engaging in it. 1 Corinthians 2:11-16, LEB

1 Peter 4:3-4 Updated American Standard Version (UASV)

³ For the time that has passed *was* sufficient *to do what the Gentiles desire to do*, having lived in licentiousness, *evil* desires, drunkenness, carousing, drinking parties, and wanton idolatries, ⁴ with respect to which they are surprised *when* you do not run with *them* into the same flood of dissipation, *and so they* revile *you.*¹²⁶

The **third greatest obstacle** is **Satan the Devil and his demon army.** Yes, they are so powerful that one demon could kill hundreds of thousands of humans in very short order. That is why true Christians receive a hedge placed around them by God, protecting them from Satan and the demons. Yes, God's servants receive special protection from this powerful force. (Job 1-2) The only way to weaken that protection is to violate your conscience repeatedly, toy with demonic activities, like horror movies, rap and heavy metal music, games like the wigi-board or dungeons and dragons.

Our human imperfections and the world that caters to them is with us 24/7. True, we can get control over our vessel by putting on the new personality, gaining the mind of Christ, and the help of Holy Spirit. However, it does not take much to drift away, fall away, refuse, draw away, become sluggish, become hardened through deceptive powers, or shrink back from Christian responsibilities. We just need to entertain the wrong thoughts too long, without dismissing them, and then we are on our way. (James 1:14-15) Now, as far as Satan goes, Peter warns us in the

---

¹²⁶ **"4:3 lewdness . . . abominable idolatries.** Lewdness describes unbridled, unrestrained sin, an excessive indulgence in sensual pleasure. Revelries has the idea of an orgy. The Greek word was used in extrabiblical literature to refer to a band of drunken, wildly acting people, swaggering and staggering through public streets, wreaking havoc. Thus, the pleasures of the ungodly are described here from the perspective of God as despicable acts of wickedness. Though Peter's readers had indulged in such sins before salvation, they must never do so again. Sin in the believer is a burden which afflicts him rather than a pleasure which delights him.

4:4 they think it strange. One's former friends are surprised, offended, and resentful because of the Christian's lack of interest in ungodly pleasures. the same flood of dissipation. Dissipation refers to the state of evil in which a person thinks about nothing else. The picture here is of a large crowd running together in a mad, wild race—a melee pursuing sin." – MacArthur, John (2005-05-09). The MacArthur Bible Commentary (Kindle Locations 64155-64162). Thomas Nelson. Kindle Edition.

extreme to, "Be sober; be on the alert. Your adversary the devil walks around like a roaring lion, looking for someone to devour." (1 Pet. 5:8) Paul also said that were to,

Ephesians 6:11-12 Updated American Standard Version (UASV)

[11] Put on the full armor of God, so that you will be able to stand firm against the schemes of the devil.[127] [12] For our struggle[128] is not against flesh and blood, but against the rulers, against the powers, against the world-rulers of this darkness, against the wicked spirit forces in the heavenly places.[129]

Threefold Assistance

There is a threefold defense against this threefold opposition to our walking with God. **First,** we have **the Word of God,** which should come in

---

[127] "**6:11 Put on the whole armor of God.** Put on conveys the idea of permanence, indicating that armor should be the Christian's sustained, life-long attire. Paul uses the common armor worn by Roman soldiers as the analogy for the believer's spiritual defense and affirms its necessity if one is to hold his position while under attack. **wiles.** This is the Greek word for schemes, carrying the idea of cleverness, crafty methods, cunning, and deception. Satan's schemes are propagated through the evil world system over which he rules, and are carried out by his demon hosts. Wiles is all-inclusive, encompassing every sin, immoral practice, false theology, false religion, and worldly enticement. See note on 2 Corinthians 2:11. **the devil.** Scripture refers to him as "the anointed cherub" (Ezek. 28:14), "the ruler of the demons" (Luke 11:15), "the god of this world" (2 Cor. 4:4), and "the prince of the power of the air" (2:2). Scripture depicts him opposing God's work (Zech. 3:1), perverting God's Word (Matt. 4:6), hindering God's servant (1 Thess. 2:18), obscuring the gospel (2 Cor. 4:4), snaring the righteous (1 Tim. 3:7), and holding the world in his power (1 John 5:19)." —MacArthur, John (2005-05-09). *The MacArthur Bible Commentary* (Kindle Locations 57495-57498). Thomas Nelson. Kindle Edition.

[128] Lit., "wrestling."

[129] "**6:12 wrestle.** A term used of hand-to-hand combat. Wrestling features trickery and deception, like Satan and his hosts when they attack. Coping with deceptive temptation requires truth and righteousness. The four designations describe the different strata and rankings of those demons and the evil supernatural empire in which they operate. Satan's forces of darkness are highly structured for the most destructive purposes. Cf. Colossians 2:15; 1 Peter 3:22. **not . . . against flesh and blood.** See 2 Corinthians 10:3–5. **spiritual hosts of wickedness.** This possibly refers to the most depraved abominations, including such things as extreme sexual perversions, occultism, and Satan worship. See note on Colossians 1:16. **in the heavenly places.** As in 1:3; 3:10, this refers to the entire realm of spiritual beings. – MacArthur, John (2005-05-09). *The MacArthur Bible Commentary* (Kindle Locations 57499-57505). Thomas Nelson. Kindle Edition.

the way of literal translations, like the English Standard Version and New American Standard Bible. Jehovah God gave us this special revelation to guide us through this wicked time. It has the power to make us stronger spiritually, as well as fortify us to accomplish his will and purposes. The Bible should be read daily, in conjunction with our recommended Bible reading program.[130] We also need to use our Bible in all of our religious meetings. If a Scripture is being read, we need to look it up. We also need to use our Bible in our ministry, meaning that we need to formulate texts that can help us to teach others the good news of the Kingdom.

Deuteronomy 17:19 Updated American Standard Version (UASV)

[19] And it shall be with him, and he shall read in it all the days of his life, that he may learn to fear Jehovah his God by keeping all the words of this law and these statutes, and doing them,

As we work our way through the Bible in our Bible reading program, let us not rush, but make sure we understand the author's intended meaning, and how we can apply that in our lives, as well as share it with others. We should be able to see our walking with God, come to life through the historical accounts found all throughout Scripture.

Joshua 1:7-8 Updated American Standard Version (UASV)

[7] Only be strong and very courageous, being careful to do according to all the law that Moses my servant commanded you; do not turn from it to the right or to the left, so that you may have success wherever you go. [8] This Book of the Law shall not depart from your mouth, but you shall meditate on it day and night, so that you may be careful to do according to all that is written in it; for then you will make your way prosperous, and then you will have good success.

Below in Psalm 1:1-3, you will notice in verse 1 that there is a progression of intimacy through walking in the counsel of the wicked, to standing with sinners, to sitting with scoffers. Each level is a sign of spending more time with, being more deeply involved. We should not be involved with any of these three, because this would never be in harmony with a Christian, who is walking with God. Yes, verse 2 helps us to appreciate where our delight is found, the law of Jehovah, to which we read and study in a meditative way, day and night, which simply means on a regular basis. Truly, verse 3 helps us to appreciate the result of avoiding certain ones, and cultivating a love for God's Word, endurance and a strong spiritual health. If we follow the counsel of verses 1-2, we will be able to weather any storm that may come upon us.

---

[130] http://christianway.us/page/bible-reading-program

Psalm 1:1-3 Updated American Standard Version (UASV)

The Way of the Righteous and the Wicked

1 Blessed is the man
   who walks not in the counsel of the wicked,
 nor stands in the way of sinners,
 nor sits in the seat of scoffers;
² but his delight is in the law of Jehovah,
 and on his law he meditates day and night.

   ³ He is like a tree
 planted by streams of water[131]
 that yields its fruit in its season,
 and its leaf does not wither.
In all that he does, he prospers.

Second, along with God's Word, are some of the best **Bible study tools** as well as the **Christian congregation**. Paul tells the Ephesians, "Look carefully then how you walk, not as unwise but as wise, making the best use of the time, because the days are evil." (Eph. 5:15-16) Moreover, the Apostle Paul exhorted "let us consider how to stir up one another to love and good works, not neglecting to meet together, as is the habit of some, but encouraging one another, and all the more as you see the Day drawing near." (Heb. 10:24-25)

Third, we have **Holy Spirit**, which sustains us in these difficult days. We need to "Live by the Spirit and reject the deeds of the flesh." If we are to be victorious over our fallen flesh, or fallen imperfection, it will be by way of the Spirit. From our first step of entering the path of salvation, to the continuation of walking on that path of developing our new personality, and taking on the mind of Christ, that is sanctification, we are in need of the Holy Spirit.

Galatians 5:16-26 Updated American Standard Version (UASV)

¹⁶ 16 But I say, walk by the Spirit, and you will not carry out the desire of the flesh. ¹⁷ For the desires of the flesh are against the Spirit, and the desires of the Spirit are against the flesh, for these are opposed to each other, so that you may not do the things you want to do. ¹⁸ But if you are led by the Spirit, you are not under the law. ¹⁹ Now the works of the flesh are evident, which are: sexual immorality, impurity, sensuality, ²⁰ idolatry, sorcery, enmity, strife, jealousy, fits of anger, rivalries, dissensions, divisions,

---

[131] "Here, David is referring to a tree that has been deliberately planted in a choice location; not something, that by chance, has sprung up just anywhere. Consideration and thought has gone into its planting. Such is the planning by God for the life of a Christian."—Bruce Prince.

²¹ envy, drunkenness, orgies, and things like these. I warn you, as I warned you before, that those who do such things will not inherit the kingdom of God. ²² But the fruit of the Spirit is love, joy, peace, patience, kindness, goodness, faithfulness, ²³ gentleness, self-control; against such things there is no law. ²⁴ And those who belong to Christ Jesus have crucified the flesh with its passions and desires.

²⁵ If we live by the Spirit, let us also walk by the Spirit. ²⁶ Let us not become conceited, provoking one another, envying one another.

Those who follow the flesh will reap the results of such a course by having unattractive fruits. On the other hand, those who follow the lead of the Spirit will have fruitage that is attractive and beneficial for themselves, family, congregation, friends, and neighbors. One thing that we have to realize by looking at other related texts is, these fruits are not the results of our efforts, are the consequence of having an active faith in Christ, which makes us receptive to them.

Godly Devotion

If we are to walk with God, we need to possess the most important ingredient, FAITH. "Now faith is the reality of what is hoped for, the proof of what is not seen." (Heb. 11:1, HCSB) "Now without faith it is impossible to please God, for the one who draws near to Him must believe that He exists and rewards those who seek Him." (Heb. 11:6, HCSB) However, before we can have the faith that we need to walk with God, we must ask, "Do two walk together unless they have met?" (Amos 3:3, LEB) Yes, if we are to truly going to get to walk with God, we must, "this is eternal life: that they may know You, the only true God, and the One You have sent, Jesus Christ." – John 17:3, HCSB.

Proverbs 2:1-6 Updated American Standard Version (UASV)

The Value of Wisdom

2 My son, if you receive my words
and treasure up my commandments with you,
² making your ear attentive to wisdom
and inclining your heart to <u>discernment</u>;¹³²
³ For if you cry for <u>discernment</u>¹³³
and raise your voice for understanding,
⁴ if you seek it like silver

---

¹³² The Hebrew word rendered here as "discernment" (*tevunah*) is related to the word *binah*, translated "understanding." Both appear at Proverbs 2:3.

¹³³ See 2.2 ftn.

and search for it as for hidden treasures,
⁵ then you will understand the fear of Jehovah
    and find the knowledge of God.
⁶ For Jehovah gives wisdom;
    from his mouth come knowledge and understanding;

Once we have studied to the point of coming to know God through knowledge, discernment, and understanding, we will begin to appreciate who he is, what he did for us, and after we had rebelled, what he did to save us. Moreover, after we have begun to live by the principles within his revelation to us, we will begin to love and appreciate him even more, as we see a life of chaos; become a life of order, blessing, and joy, even in this imperfect world. If we are truly to walk with God, we must be in harmony with his will and purposes. "Not everyone who says to me, 'Lord, Lord,' will enter the kingdom of heaven, but the one who does the will of my Father who is in heaven." (Matt 7:21, ESV) Exactly, what is the will and purpose of God? You might be thinking that it is to remove sin and death from his human creation, because of sending his Son, Jesus Christ to ransom those that are receptive to the Gospel. However, this is not the primary purpose of God; it is the vindication of the slanderous accusations made by Satan the Devil, made in the Garden of Eden, and in the book of Job. (Gen 3:1-6; Job 1-2) It is by means of his Son in the Kingdom of God that is to bring this about. The secondary purpose, which runs alongside is the vindication of his human creation.

Exodus 34:14 Updated American Standard Version (UASV)

¹⁴ for you shall worship no other god, for Jehovah, whose name is Jealous, is a jealous God,[134]

Mark 12:30 Updated American Standard Version (UASV)

³⁰ and you shall love the Lord your God with all your heart, and with all your soul, and with all your mind, and with all your strength.'[135]

---

[134] God is jealous for His people Israel in sense (1), that is, God is intolerant of rival gods (Exod. 20:5; 34:14; Deut. 4:24; 5:9) One expression of God's jealousy for Israel is God's protection of His people from enemies. Thus God's jealousy includes avenging Israel (Ezek. 36:6; 39:25; Nah. 1:2; Zech. 1:14; 8:2). Phinehas is described as jealous with God's jealousy (Num. 25:11, 13, sometimes translated zealous for God). Elijah is similarly characterized as jealous (or zealous) for God (1 Kings 19:10, 14). *Holman Illustrated Bible Dictionary*, ed. Chad Brand, Charles Draper, Archie England et al. (Nashville, TN: Holman Bible Publishers, 2003), 873.

[135] Quotation from Deuteronomy 6:4–5, which reads, "Hear, O Israel! Jehovah our God is one Jehovah! You shall love Jehovah your God with all your heart and with all your soul and with all your might."

Matthew 6:33 Updated American Standard Version (UASV)

³³ But be you seeking¹³⁶ the kingdom of God and his righteousness, and all these things will be added to you.

Have we grown so close to God that we understand the issues behind why we were allowed to enter into this period of sin and death, as opposed to just removing those that caused the rebellion, why he has allowed pain and suffering to continue for so long?¹³⁷ Are we willing to work toward the same purpose, the vindication of God's great name and reputation, to resolve the issues that were raised? If so, we will seek out what our role in the great commission is (Matt. 28:19-20), and we will carry it out with our whole heart, soul, mind and strength.

God's Case for Justice

If we are to walk with God, we have to be guided by his divine justice. He is holy, so we to must be holy, which means that like him, we separate ourselves from anything that would be at odds with his moral standards. In addition, while he is perfect in an absolute sense, we can do this by loving our enemies and praying for those who persecute us. Even though we are truly insignificant as we walk alongside the Creator of all things, we must be a dispenser of his brand of justice. – Micah 6:8; 1 Peter 1:16; Matthew 5:48.

We must love to do right,¹³⁸ but deplore the idea of ever doing what is bad, if we are to continue our walk with God. Satan's world has catered to the fleshly desires that lie within each of us for so long; it is not great thing for us to be tempted in a weak moment, and surrender. Therefore, our best recourse is to cultivate abhorrence for what is bad. Not one of us should ever believe that we are too strong, or that we might never stumble, because the Apostle Paul was not so bold to believe this about himself. – Isaiah 61:8; Psalm 45:7; 97:10; Romans 12:9; 1 Corinthians 9:27; 10:12.

Each of us is well aware of what our particular weakness is. The best defense against any such weakness is to identify it to ourselves outwardly in prayer, regularly. We need to understand how we fall short in this weakness, what is usually going on with us at the time we give in. We need

---

¹³⁶ Gr., *zeteite;* the verb form indicates continuous action.

¹³⁷ Why Has God Permitted Wickedness and Suffering:

http://www.christianpublishers.org/suffering-evil-why-god

¹³⁸ "The Greek word "agape", which is generally translated into the all-rounder English word "love", means simply to seek the other's highest good. We can do this even for those who persecute us."—Bruce Prince.

to see if there are innocent- appearing situations that will put us in the line of fire. Once these are understood, we need to avoid them at all costs. If one is an alcoholic, it is all too clear that he would not take a job as a bartender, or rent an apartment above a bar. However, what about the convenient store where you pick up the newspaper, if it has a very large alcohol section. If our weakness has something to do with sex, we would not want to find ourselves in a compromising situation with the opposite sex, or the same sex if this is the tendency. If immoral thoughts enter our mind, they are to be immediately dismissed ("flee fornication"), followed by a prayer. We must self-talk to ourselves about the consequences, quashing all irrational thoughts. – Matthew 10:26; 2 Cor. 10:5; Isa. 52:11.

Love Kindness

If we are to walk with God, we must love kindness. The Hebrew word *checed*, is rendered "loving-kindness, steadfast love, grace, mercy, faithfulness, goodness, devotion." "This word is used 240 times in the Old Testament, and is especially frequent in the Psalter. The term is one of the most important in the vocabulary of Old Testament theology and ethics."[139] If it were not for God's loving kindness toward his creation, at the rebellion, we would not even be here having this conversation. The Psalmist says, "How precious is your steadfast love, O God! The children of mankind take refuge in the shadow of your wings." (Ps. 26:7) Jeremiah helps us to appreciate that 'in Jehovah God is salvation." (Lam. 3:22-23) And James, the half-brother of Jesus wrote, "the Lord is compassionate and merciful." – James 5:11.

The Apostle Paul gives us the fruitage of the Spirit, "**love**, joy, peace, patience, **kindness**, goodness, faithfulness, gentleness, [and] self-control." If we can take on the quality of Loving-kindness, we will be more sympathetic, empathetic, tolerant, thoughtful, tender and supportive of others, even enemies. When we enter into a difficulty with another, we will have the ability to identify with and understand their feelings or difficulties. Even though it may appear that Jehovah God is far removed from us and our circumstances, he is very much able to identify with our circumstances, especially since he sent his Son to walk in our shoes, so to speak.

Psalm 103:6-14 Updated American Standard Version (UASV)

---

[139] W. E. Vine, Merrill F. Unger and William White, Jr., vol. 1, *Vine's Complete Expository Dictionary of Old and New Testament Words* (Nashville, TN: T. Nelson, 1996), 142.

⁶ Jehovah performs righteous deeds
   and judgments for all who are oppressed.
⁷ He made known his ways to Moses,
   his acts to the sons of Israel.
⁸ Jehovah is compassionate and gracious,
   slow to anger and abounding in lovingkindness.
⁹ He will not always find fault,
   nor will he keep his anger forever.
¹⁰ He does not deal with us according to our sins,
   nor repaid us according to our iniquities.
¹¹ For as high as the heavens are above the earth,
   So great is his lovingkindness toward those who fear him.
¹² As far as the east is from the west,
   so far does he remove our transgressions from us.
¹³ As a father has compassion on his children,
   so Jehovah has compassion on those who fear him.
¹⁴ For he himself knows our formation;
   he remembers that we are dust.

Jesus Christ was the perfect example of an empathetic person. He chose to give up his position in heaven, to come down here and suffer with us, to walk with us, suffer a severe persecution, and a horrendous execution. Remember that Saul (Paul), prior to his conversion was persecuting the Christians and even played a part in the stoning of Stephen. The risen Christ came to Paul on the road to Damascus, as he was heading to arrest more Christians. Paul said to Jesus, "Who are you, Lord?" And he said, "I am Jesus, whom you are persecuting! (Acts 9:5) Jesus' statement means that he was putting himself in the place of those who were being persecuted. In other words, to be persecuting them, was the same as persecuting him.

Once Saul became a Christian, and started using his name Paul, we find him imitating Jesus empathic example. Paul too put himself in the circumstances of those to whom he witnessed.

1 Corinthians 9:19-23 Updated American Standard Version (UASV)

¹⁹ For though I am free from all men, I have made myself a slave to all, so that I may gain more. ²⁰ And so to the Jews I became as a Jew, that I might gain Jews; to those under the law I became as under the law, though I myself am not under the law, that I might gain those under the law. ²¹ To those without law I became as without law, although I am not without law toward God but under the law toward Christ, that I might gain those without law. ²² To the weak I became weak, that I might gain the weak. I have become all things to all men, that I might by all means save

some. [23] But I do all things for the sake of the gospel, that I may become a fellow partaker of it.

Walk Humbly With Your God

Imagine that the Creator of everything is willing to humble himself to walk with us. One would think that is a given (common sense) that, we would humble ourselves to walk with him. What exactly is involved in our humbling ourselves? It means that we are obedient to him as the sovereign of the universe. This should be the first thing we learn before we ever commit ourselves to him. If we are humble in our dealing, we will not be self-important. This means that a wife would recognize the headship of her husband, and that the congregation would recognize the authority of those taking the lead among them. Let us suppose that the wife of a household has better judgment than her husband has. It does not mean that she usurps his position, but then again, it does not mean that the husband is dismissive of her counsel. She can inform him, and he makes the decision based on that added knowledge.

Humility helps us to be submissive to those that have been given responsibility over us. The one with the responsibility could be a husband, a pastor in the congregation, or the superior authorities of the nation where we live. Everyone has someone who is over him or her but God. We need to keep in mind that our greatest goal is to make peace where there may be none, or to preserve peace. Another concern is our unity as a family or as a Christian congregation. Therefore, we must be wise in our dealings with others, considering much beside ourselves. If we have insight that can improve a family decision, or the congregation, it should be given at the appropriate time, and in the right way.

Certainly, if you have ever investigated the Bible a even a little, you know that the wisest course is to walk with God. However, if you have been at it for some time, you may have discovered that it is not always easy to do, when based on your human weaknesses, the wicked world that we live in, in addition to the influence of Satan and his demons. However, we know that it is not too difficult for God, who has given us his **(1)** Word, **(2)** study tools and the Christian congregation, as well as **(3)** the Holy Spirit. Then, he has opened himself up to hearing our every prayer that is in harmony with his will and purposes, giving us a chance to talk with him, especially in time of need.

Review Questions

- What does it mean to walk humbly with your God?

- What threefold resistance to we come across in our walk with our God?

- What threefold assistance do we have in our walk with our God

- What is Godly devotion?

- What do we mean by God's case for justice?

- What does it mean to love kindness?

- What does it mean to walk humbly with your God?

OTHER Books By Edward D. Andrews

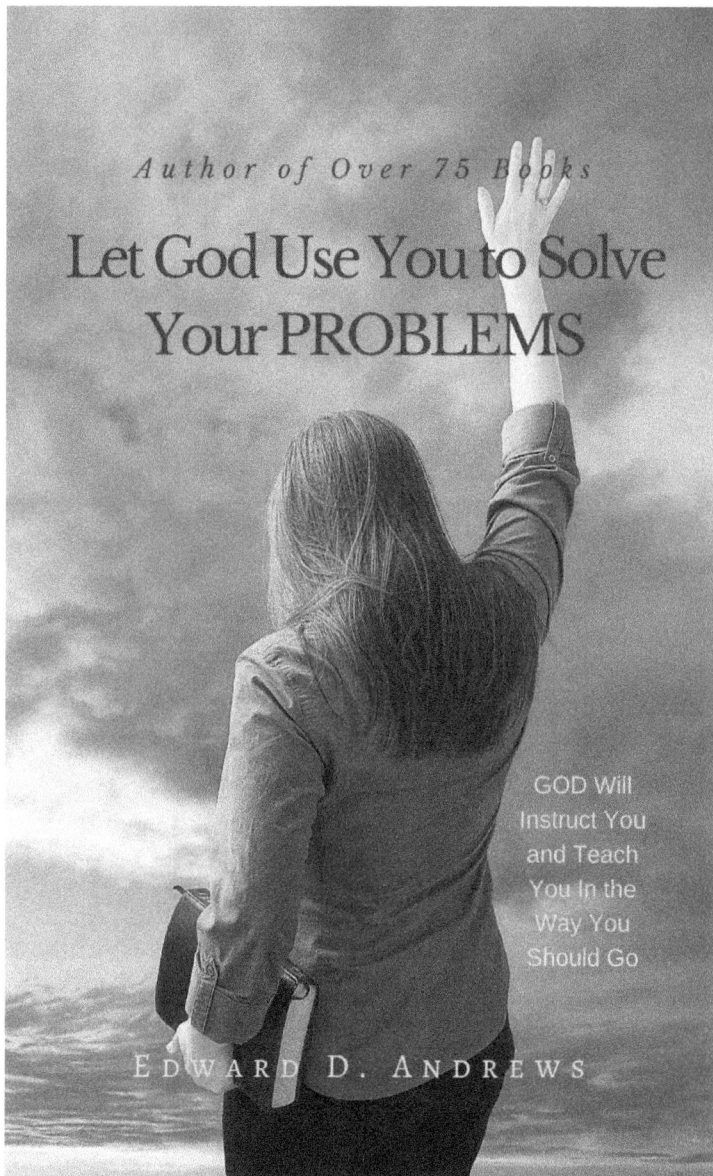

Christian Publishing House

ISBN-13: 978-1-945757-86-0

ISBN-10: 1-945757-86-8

GOD WILL GET YOU THROUGH THIS

Hope and Help for Your Difficult Times

EDWARD D. ANDREWS

Christian Publishing House
ISBN-13: 978-1-945757-72-3

ISBN-10: 1-945757-72-8

FEARLESS

Be Courageous and Strong Through Your Faith In These Last Days

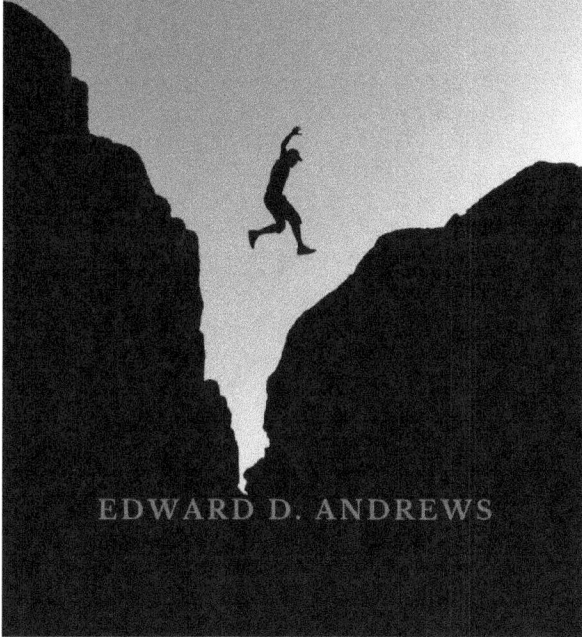

EDWARD D. ANDREWS

Christian Publishing House

ISBN-13: 978-1-945757-69-3

ISBN-10: 1-945757-69-8

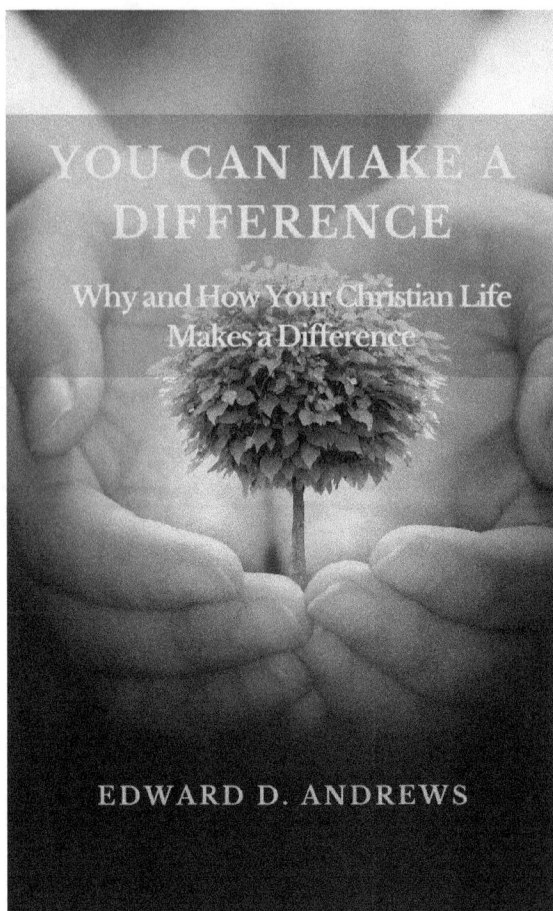

YOU CAN MAKE A DIFFERENCE

DIFFERENCE

Why and How Your Christian Life
Makes a Difference

EDWARD D. ANDREWS

Christian Publishing House

ISBN-13: 978-1-945757-74-7

ISBN-10: 1-945757-74-4

Bible Principles

TURN OLD HABITS INTO NEW HABITS

Why and How the Bible
Makes a Difference

EDWARD D. ANDREWS

Christian Publishing House
ISBN-13: 978-1-945757-73-0

ISBN-10: 1-945757-73-6

Bibliography

Anders, Max. *Holman New Testament Commentary: vol. 8, Galatians, Ephesians, Philippians, Colossians.* Nashville, TN: Broadman & Holman Publishers, 1999.

Anderson, Neil T. *Discipleship Counseling: The Complete Guide to Helping Others: Walk in Freedon and Gow in Christ.* Ventura: Regal Books, 2003.

Andrews, Edward D. *FOR AS I THINK IN MY HEART—SO I AM: Combining Biblical Counseling with Cognitive Behavioral Therapy.* Cambridge: Christian Publishing House, 2013.

—. *PUT OFF THE OLD PERSON WITH ITS PRACTICES And Put On the New Person.* Cambridge: Christian Publishing House, 2014.

Andrews, Stephen J, and Robert D Bergen. *Holman Old Testament Commentary: 1-2 Samuel.* Nashville: Broadman & Holman, 2009.

Arndt, William, Frederick W. Danker, and Walter Bauer. *A Greek-English Lexicon of the New Testament and Other Early Christian Literature.* 3rd ed. . Chicago: University of Chicago Press, 2000.

Arnold, Clinton E. *Zondervan Illustrated Bible Backgrounds Commentary: Matthew, Mark, Luke, vol. 1.* Grand Rapids, MI: Zondervan, 2002.

Barry, John D., and Lazarus Wentz. *The Lexham Bible Dictionary.* Bellingham, WA: Logos Bible Software, 2012.

Benner, David G. *Strategic Pastoral Counseling: A Short-Term Structural Model.* Grand Rapids: Baker Academic, 1992, 2003.

Bercot, David W. *A Dictionary of Early Christian Beliefs.* Peabody: Hendrickson, 1998.

Black, David Alan. *IT"S STILL GREEK TO ME: An Easy-to-Understand Guide t Intermediate Greek.* Grand Rapids: Baker Books, 1998.

Bland, Dave. *The College Press NIV Commentary: Proverbs, Ecclesiastes & Song of Songs, .* Joplin: College Press Pub. Co., 2002.

Boa, Kenneth, and William Kruidenier. *Holman New Testament Commentary: Romans, Vol. 6.* Nashville, TN: Broadman & Holman, 2000.

Boisen, Sean, Mark Keaton, Jeremy Thompson, and David Witthoff. *Bible Sense Lexicon.* Bellingham: Lexham Press, June 25, 2014.

Brand, Chad, Charles Draper, and England Archie. *Holman Illustrated Bible Dictionary: Revised, Updated and Expanded.* Nashville, TN: Holman, 2003.

Bromiley, Geoffrey W. *The International Standard Bible Encyclopedia (Vol. 1-4).* Grand Rapids, MI: William B. Eerdmans Publishing Co., 1986.

Bromiley, Geoffrey W., and Gerhard Friedrich. *Theological Dictionary of the New Testament, ed. Gerhard Kittel, vol. 4.* Grand Rapids, MI: Eerdmans, 1964-.

Calloway, Brent A. *THE BOOK OF JAMES: CPH CHRISTIAN LIVING COMMENTARY.* Cambridge: Chriwstian Publishing House, 2015.

Clinton, Tim, and George Ohlschlager. *Competent Christian Counseling; Volume One: Foundations and Practice of Compassionate Soul Care.* Colorado Springs, CO: WaterBrook Press, 2008.

Cooper, Rodney. *Holman New Testament Commentary: Mark.* Nashville: Broadman & Holman Publishers, 2000.

Easton, M. G. *Easton's Bible Dictionary.* Oak Harbor, WA: Logos Research Systems, 1996, c1897.

Edwards, Tyron. *A Dictionary of Thoughts.* Detroit: F. B. Dickerson Company, 1908.

Elwell, Walter A. *Baker Encyclopedia of the Bible.* Grand Rapids: Baker Book House, 1988.

—. *Evangelical Dictionary of Theology (Second Edition).* Grand Rapids: Baker Academic, 2001.

Elwell, Walter A, and Philip Wesley Comfort. *Tyndale Bible Dictionary.* Wheaton, Ill: Tyndale House Publishers, 2001.

Freedman, David Noel, Allen C. Myers, and Astrid B. Beck. *Eerdmans Dictionary of the Bible .* Grand Rapids, Mich.: W.B. Eerdmans , 2000.

Gangel, Kenneth O. *Holman New Testament Commentary: Acts.* Nashville, TN: Broadman & Holman Publishers, 1998.

Gangel, Kenneth O. *Holman New Testament Commentary, vol. 4, John .* Nashville, TN: Broadman & Holman Publishers, 2000.

Garland, David E. *1 Corinthians, Baker Exegetical Commentary on the New Testament.* Grand Rapids, MI: : Baker Academic, 2003.

Green, Joel B, Scot McKnight, and Howard Marshall. *Dictionary of Jesus and the Gospels.* Downers Grove, IL: InterVarsity Press, 1992.

Guralnik, David B. *Webster's New World Dictionary, 2d college ed.* New York, NY: Simon and Schuster, 1984.

Hastings, James, John A Selbie, and John C Lambert. *A Dictionary of Christ and the Gospels.* New York, NY: Charles Scribner's Sons, 1907.

Hendriksen, William. *Baker New Testament Commentary: Matthew.* Grand Rapids: Baker Book House, 1973.

Kittel, Gerhard, Gerhard Friedrich, and Geoffrey William Bromiley. *Theological Dictionary of the New Testament.* Grand Rapids: Eerdmans, 1995, c1985.

Kollar, Charles Allen. *Solution-Focused Pastoral Counseling: An Effective Short-Term Approach for Getting People Back on Track.* Grand Rapids: Zondervan, 1997.

Larson, Knute. *Holman New Testament Commentary, vol. 9, I & II Thessalonians, I & II Timothy, Titus, Philemon.* Nashville, TN: Broadman & Holman Publishers, 2000.

Lea, Thomas D. *Holman New Testament Commentary: Vol. 10, Hebrews, James.* Nashville, TN: Broadman & Holman Publishers, 1999.

Lukaszewski, Albert L., Mark Dubis, and Ted J Blakley. *The Lexham Syntactic Greek New Testament.* Bellingham: Logos Bible Software, 2013.

MacArthur, John. *Counseling: How to Counsel Biblically.* Nashville, TN: Thomas Nelson, Inc., 2005.

—. *The MacArthur Bible Commentary.* Nashville: Thomas Nelson, 2005.

Marshall, Alfred. *THE NASB-NIV INTERLINEAR GREEK-ENGLISH NEW TESTAMENT.* Grand Rapids: Zondervan, 1993.

McMinn, Mark R. *Psychology, Theology, and Spirituality in Christian Counseling (AACC Library).* Carol Stream, IL: Tyndale House Publishers, 2010.

Microsoft. *Encarta ® World English Dictionary.* Redmond: Microsoft Corporation, 1998-2010.

Mirriam-Webster, Inc. *Mirriam-Webster's Collegiate Dictionary. Eleventh Edition.* Springfield: Mirriam-Webster, Inc., 2003.

Morris, Leon. *The Gospel According to Matthew.* Grand Rapids, MI: Inter-Varsity Press, 1992.

Mounce, William D. *Mounce's Complete Expository Dictionary of Old & New Testament Words.* Grand Rapids, MI: Zondervan, 2006.

Myers, Allen C. *The Eerdmans Bible Dictionary* . Grand Rapids, Mich: Eerdmans, 1987.

Pratt Jr, Richard L. *Holman New Testament Commentary: I & II Corinthians, vol. 7.* Nashville: Broadman & Holman Publishers, 2000.

Swanson, James. *A Dictionary of Biblical Languages - Greek.* Washington: Logos Research Systems, 1997.

Vine, W E. *Vine's Expository Dictionary of Old and New Testament Words.* Nashville: Thomas Nelson, 1996.

Walls, David, and Max Anders. *Holman New Testament Commentary: I & II Peter, I, II & III John, Jude.* Nashville: Broadman & Holman Publishers, 1996.

Weber, Stuart K. *Holman New Testament Commentary, vol. 1, Matthew.* Nashville, TN: Broadman & Holman Publishers, 2000.

Whitney, Donald S. *Spiritual Disciplines for the Christian Life with Bonus Content (Pilgrimage Growth Guide).* Colorado Springs, CO: Navpress, 1991.

Wilkins, Michael, and Craig A. Evans. *The Gospels and Acts (The Holman Apologetics Commentary on the Bible).* Nashville: B & H Publishing Group, 2013.

Wood, D R W. *New Bible Dictionary (Third Edition).* Downers Grove: InterVarsity Press, 1996.

Zodhiates, Spiros. *The Complete Word Study Dictionary: New Testament.* Chattanooga: AMG Publishers, 2000, c1992, c1993.

www.ingramcontent.com/pod-product-compliance
Lightning Source LLC
LaVergne TN
LVHW051347080426
835509LV00020BA/3327